dot-for

dot-font
talking about fonts

JOHN D. BERRY

MARK BATTY PUBLISHER

Dot-font: Talking About Fonts
© 2006 by John D. Berry

DESIGN & PRODUCTION: John D. Berry
TYPEFACES USED: MVB Verdigris (*text*); HTF Whitney (*display and small display*); and Freight (*display on cover*).
COVER IMAGE: "ABC & XYZ" (2001). Designed & letterpress printed by Christopher Stern. Co-written by Christopher Stern & Jules Remedios Faye. Limited Edition of 50. Used by permission.

Photograph of Robert Norton (page 88) copyright by Dana J. Anderson. Used by permission.

Every effort has been made to trace accurate ownership of copyrighted text and visual materials used in this book. Errors or omissions will be corrected in subsequent editions, provided notification is sent to the publisher.

Library of Congress Control Number:
2006933334

Printed and bound at the National Press
The Hashemite Kingdom of Jordan

10 9 8 7 6 5 4 3 2 1   FIRST EDITION

This edition © 2006
Mark Batty Publisher
36 West 37th Street, Penthouse
New York NY 10018

www.markbattypublisher.com

ISBN-10: 0-9772827-0-8
ISBN-13: 978-09772827-0-8

Contents

DEDICATION
To my partner Eileen Gunn
for continually asking the hardest questions

ACKNOWLEDGMENTS
Thanks to Creativepro (*www.creativepro.com*), for providing the platform on which all of these articles were published, and through which they reached their first audience. In particular, thanks to my editors there: Pamela Pfiffner, Mitt Jones, and Terri Stone. Thanks, too, to Peter Fraterdeus, for graciously letting me use the name "dot-font" without restriction, after having unrealized plans to use it himself. And thanks to all the people I've written about, for doing interesting things.

Thanks to Buzz Poole, Jacob Albert, and Christopher Salyers at Mark Batty Publisher, who all helped to make this book what it is.

Thanks to Chris Stern & Jules Faye, for use of the remarkable image from one of Chris's broadsides that is reproduced on the cover of this book. And to everybody who supplied images, either for the original columns or for this book — especially to Dave Farey, Larry Brady, Gerard Unger, Andrew Pennock, and the Enschedé Font Foundry, who came up with images when asked at the very last minute.

Thanks to Mark van Bronkhorst, Jonathan Hoefler, and Josh Darden, for the use of their fonts, respectively: MVB Verdigris (text), HTF Whitney (display), and Freight (cover display).

introduction | John D. Berry

I BEGAN WRITING the "dot-font" column for the portal website *Creativepro.com* in the summer of 2000, dealing with the ongoing changes in the world of type and typography and putting them into perspective. The essays in this book were all published on Creativepro, originally to a weekly deadline and later at a slightly more relaxed pace. I wrote them for the general community of people interested in type and graphic design, and for anyone who might either be using type or be curious about it. In that time, the column has attracted a certain following.

The essays in this book all concern themselves, to one degree or another, with fonts: that is to say, in older parlance, with typefaces. For the most part, I've excluded from this book essays about how to use type, or about graphic design and design in general. The nature of these essays makes it hard to draw any hard-and-fast line and say, "*These* are about this topic; *those* are about something else." A companion volume, *Dot-font: Talking About Design*, deals with more general questions of design, graphic and otherwise; and a later volume will focus on how type is used: i.e., typography. But the focus of this particular selection is definitely and explicitly on fonts — what they are, how they work, what they're good for, and a glance at quite a few specific fonts in concrete detail.

While I've removed the most ephemeral topical bits, keep in mind that all of these essays were originally written for immediate publication at a particular moment. References to what someone was up to in 2001, for example, or what they meant to do next, may now be woefully out of date, but in some cases I've left them in, to convey the sense of immediacy that they had when they were first published.

Not everything I wrote on a quick schedule merits reprinting, of course, but the essays in this book seemed to have a value beyond their moment of composition. Within each section, the book is arranged chronologically, with the date of first publication at the beginning of each essay. You may read them right through in order, or you may pick and choose. Together, they constitute a kaleidoscopic snapshot of the art and craft of type, at the start of the 21st century.

Here they are, in your hand.

tradition

Type under the knife

Some of our digital letters began life as stencils cut by hand out of bits of red plastic, which were used to create the rub-down lettering marketed in the '60s by Letraset.

[*June 19, 2000*]

MIKE PARKER has been in the type business for a long time; he co-founded Bitstream with Matthew Carter, and before that he ran the type-development program at Mergenthaler Linotype, in the days of hot metal and early phototype. The last time I saw Mike, I was telling him about how the Type Directors Club had just given their medal to Colin Brignall, in London a couple of weeks back. When I pointed out that Colin had started at Letraset in 1964 and mentioned that I was planning to write about the changes in type technology and marketing that Colin's career had encompassed, Mike nodded and said: "That period includes pretty much all of it. From hot metal to phototype to digital type to PostScript — it's all happened in the last forty years." In the case of Colin Brignall and Letraset, that includes a unique technology that was a response to the needs of designers in the 1960s.

Why does this matter now? Because it's the context of the typographic world we live in. It helps to know where the typefaces we use come from, and why they're available in the ways they are. For designers of new typefaces today, it's useful to know how type has been made in the past — a past that's not particularly old yet.

Rub down, turn around
Things have a way of coming around full-circle. Colin Brignall became Letraset's director of typeface development in 1980, when the company was developing typefaces for release as sheets of dry-transfer ("rub-down") letters that could be literally rubbed down onto a sheet

of paper or a layout board. Twenty years later, after a few major corporate and technical upheavals, he found himself once again in charge of a program of developing new typefaces for Letraset. Only instead of rub-down letters, these new typefaces would be released as digital fonts, sold directly on the web.

At the TDC's award dinner in London, a slim booklet was distributed to each of the attendees: *Letraset & Stencil Cutting*. This booklet, originally published in 1996 by International Typeface Corporation, New York, and the St Bride Printing Library, London, gives a detailed account of the unique method by which typefaces were created for Letraset. The main text is written by Colin Brignall and Dave Farey, with shorter accounts by several participants (Mike Daines, Alan Meeks, Freda Sack, and Peter O'Donnell).

The collapse of civilization, again

As Farey and Brignall point out, when Letraset started up, it was regarded as the "new kid on the block." Dry-transfer lettering wasn't considered "real" typesetting, and critics complained that "it would destroy the 'craft of lettering' and letterspacing in the hands of the uninitiated and would compromise typographic standards." (All of which it probably did, in some of the less talented hands, just as desktop publishing did a generation later. But then, bad lettering and bad typesetting existed in the old days, too.)

Early on, to prove its seriousness, Letraset joined the Association Typographique Internationale (ATypI, the main international body of the type business) and negotiated licensing agreements with other ATypI member companies to reproduce their type designs on dry-transfer sheets. These agreements led to one of the oddest techniques ever used for duplicating a type design.

Shake, rattle, and roll

Letraset would buy a case of new type and place it in a machine along with a complicated arrangement of pressure-sensitive film and two layers of reinforced clear plastic with hundreds of ball bearings in between. When the machine was switched on, say Brignall and Farey, "The noise was deafening, and a special room had to be built to house the machine." But this bizarre method did produce accurate renditions on the film of the outlines of the metal typefaces. "These enlargements were then measured, analysed, discussed, re-measured, occasionally re-drawn, interpreted and finally, accompanied with pages of notes, overlaid with Rubylith Ulano for the process of stencil cutting to start."

A sheet of pressure-sensitive film with an image created from a case of metal type.

Cut out for type design

It was the stencil cutting that was the heart of the Letraset process. Letter designs were cut out by hand with a knife in sheets of Rubylith, which were then used as the masters for the photographic production of sheets of alphabets. "Cutting curves," say Brignall and Farey, "is done entirely freehand and begins with the knife carefully following the shape of the letter, while the other hand twists the letter to allow the cutting hand to go as far around it as possible without stopping. The skill of cutting is to know when to stop, to always make perfect joins, and not to be afraid of trimming. To be avoided at all costs is 'the dreaded peanut,' an in-out effect that occurs if the join between a straight and curved cut is anything less than perfect." It was not a craft that you could practice on a keyboard, with the reassurance of an

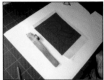

Undo command. "One of the fascinations of stencil cutting," they add, "is to watch someone do it, or to watch someone watching a stencil cutter. Involuntarily, the watcher's body language starts to mirror the cutter, the head will turn, the fingers will flex, and finally there will be an expellation of air, rather like a swimmer surfacing from under water!"

While at first the Letraset type studio was simply reproducing existing typefaces, they started issuing their own original designs as early as 1963. The company very sensibly invited their better stencil cutters to submit their own designs, since the rigorous training they had undergone in learning to cut stencils (and work with all the variety of existing typeface designs) gave them what was, quite literally, a hands-on understanding of letterforms and how they worked.

Back to the future

By the time *Letraset & Stencil Cutting* was written, the old technology had become obsolete and Letraset's type library, which became amalgated with that of ITC (another story entirely), had turned digital. The later typeface releases, under Colin Brignall's direction, included not just a host of lively display faces but also a number of striking text families by designers such as the underappreciated Michael Gills.

The process of cutting a letter by hand out of a sheet of Rubylith.

The pleasures of old type books

A 1950s book of type specimens from the Nebiolo type foundry in Italy.

In an old Nebiolo type book, Italian type design of the mid-20th century provides us with echoes of the modern and the antique.
[*May 14, 2003*]

OLD TYPE-SPECIMEN BOOKS can be a cornucopia of design ideas. One of my favorites is a casebound book I picked up years ago, called *Caratteri Nebiolo* — a specimen book of the typefaces available at the time from the Italian type foundry Nebiolo, in Torino. There's no date in the book, but it must have been published in the 1950s, judging from some of the typefaces shown. It reflects what was then both new and old: the latest releases from the foundry, and the older faces that were still in demand. All of these typefaces reflected the trends of their day; some of them helped to create the trends of the future.

Aldo Novarese's early types
Nebiolo was one of the major Italian type foundries, at a time when Italian design was on the cutting edge — though the type business, unlike some other aspects of visual communication, was quite conservative. You wouldn't know it to page through *Caratteri Nebiolo*, but the foundry employed one of the best-known modern type designers in Italy, the prolific Aldo Novarese, whose myriad typefaces have spread around the world. His most influential typeface design appears in this book (although no designer credit is given): Microgramma.

Microgramma bold extended in use.

Microgramma was a quintessentially modern typeface — not "modern" in the type-history sense, as a high-

Detail from the opening page of the Microgramma section.

contrast roman letter with a vertical axis, but modern in the 20th-century sense: streamlined, clean, sleek, stripped to its essentials. It's a sans-serif typeface built on the form of a rounded square — or rather a rectangle, slightly upright in the normal width, stretched out in the wide, and strictly narrow in the condensed. There's a bold, but the fairly light-looking regular weight defines the face — and the look of Italian modernism in print. The rounded corners and squared turns make Microgramma look like machined wire.

In digital or photo type, the flat-sided forms would make it possible (and tempting) to set the letters too close together, but these were metal types; even fitted tight, they kept enough room to breathe.

Microgramma was a purely uppercase typeface; Novarese's later extension of it into a lowercase, which was released under the name Eurostile, does not appear in this specimen book.

But other Novarese creations do, in a variety of weights and widths and styles. His Egizio, for instance, which has been much imitated, took 19th-century slab-serif display faces and introduced their lively but slightly clunky vigor into the 1950s.

Egyptian-style types from the Nebiolo collection.

Dekoration
Malesherbes
Storia Nazionale

Sample settings in graded sizes of Quirinus.

*Contrasting Microgramma with a script typeface, and using the Microgramma **M** as a graphic element.*

Part of a page showing Athenaeum in use, including one of its decorated initial caps.

Show-offs

The creators of the specimen book wanted it to be both a reference and a way to show off their type and how it might be used. Some pages simply give sample settings of words and phrases at different sizes (and in different languages, to reflect their international clientele).

Others show well-constructed pages that suggest ways to use the typeface in real-world situations. Still others show imaginative juxtapositions of different typefaces. Many of the sections of the book start with an opening page announcing the theme of the typeface. And sometimes the book designer just plain shows off, pulling out all the stops and flinging ornaments, borders, and ornamental caps into the fray.

FILIGRANE DETTE ANCHE MARCHE D'ACQUA
USATE DALL'ANTICA INDUSTRIA CARTARIA

egni o marche d'acqua è il nome corrente con cui sono designate le autentiche filigrane con le quali i maestri cartai distinguevano i propri prodotti. In che consistono? Sono in generale figure stilizzate, di sapore un po' primitivo, facili a poter essere realizzate con fili metallici sui setacci dove nasceva il foglio lavorato a mano [*].

Quante sono? Forse una risposta esatta non l'ha ancor data nessuno quantunque esistano ricche raccolte di queste innumerevoli figure che hanno fregiato le antiche carte; il loro numero è straordinariamente elevato. La conoscenza delle marche d'acqua, la loro classificazione cronologica sono di utilissima guida per lo studio degli antichi documenti; l'approfondire il significato dei vari segni, il raggrupparli secondo i paesi, le regioni, le fabbriche è studio scientifico ben utile e doveroso verso questa prodigiosa industria della carta che tanta parte ha avuto nello sviluppo della cultura nella civiltà moderna.

ANNO 1356
Clermont-Ferrand. *Archivio Municipale*

Several weights, styles, and sizes of Quirinus in practical use.

Detail from the opening page of the section on the typeface Fluidum.

A double-page spread, showing typographic borders and graphic elements as well as a variety of sizes and styles of type.

Modular book(lets)

Many of the most exuberant demonstrations of the various typefaces in use were first created as flyers or brochures to promote individual new faces. Tucked into the back of my copy of the book is a four-page, three-color specimen of a condensed version of Egizio ("Egizio stretto neretto"), combined with a showing of a script face in what they call "tipo inglese" (English copperplate style), called Juliet. These brochures could be bound into signatures for a new specimen book, or kept separate as a promotional handout.

Hands-on

At the front of the book is a short section on ordering type from Nebiolo — carefully explained in five languages. Since this was a true foundry, casting type in metal to order, the instructions on "How to Place Your Orders" include worries that would never occur to a user of digital type, such as the printing height (how tall each piece of type must be) or the weight of the metal type to be shipped: "The weights given refer to types delivered in Italian fonts and are approximate with a tolerance of plus or minus 5 to 10%. For types to be supplied in French,

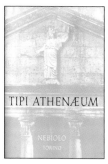

Opening page of the Athenaeum section.

Opening page showing a then-new condensed version of Aldo Novarese's typeface Egizio.

Spanish, German, English, Portuguese, Dutch, Belgian, etc. fonts, weights vary according to the font wanted."

It gives new meaning (or rather, a much older meaning) to the notion of "the weight of a font."

We don't order type in the same way today, but the printed specimens presented in this 1950s book can give us inspiration for designing with type — and send us scurrying to try and find some of these typefaces in digital form. The nature of these once-new type designs is both elusive and insistently material: it would be hard to come by most of them as metal type today, but the printed manifestation of the types in use remains.

old & new

Gail Anderson's rendering of the TDC² 2001 judges, from the TDC annual: Helen Keyes, Robert Bringhurst, Tobias Frere-Jones, and Carol Twombly.

Meeting the revivals

Where do you draw the line between copying and rendering in a new medium? Typeface revivals continually raise this question.

[*January 26, 2001*]

How do you judge the design of a typeface that is a revival of an older typeface? This question came up — not for the first time — during the judging of TDC² 2001, the New York Type Directors Club's annual type-design competition.

Sources and influences

This thorny question caused a lot of discussion among the TDC² judges. (The judges were Carol Twombly, Tobias Frere-Jones, Helen Keyes, and Robert Bringhurst. I chaired the type competition.)

Most typeface designs are based on other, earlier typefaces, to one degree or another. You could argue, in fact, that all typefaces are derivative, since they are all versions of our common Latin alphabet (or of another alphabet, common to another language and script). If a type designer didn't make shapes that were reasonably familiar, the resulting typeface wouldn't be readable. Designers delight in pushing this particular envelope, but if they leave it behind entirely, they'll find that what they're designing isn't type.

The questions that came up in New York had nothing to do with experimental type, and everything to do with type that was very familiar indeed. Several of the fonts submitted were digital versions of typefaces that had never been digitized. Can such a typeface be considered an original design? The judges weren't happy with appearing to give credit for the design to someone who had merely adapted it to the latest technology. Yet there was no question that the work, and judgment, required for such an adaptation are considerable and important, and if the result is a success, then it should be honored.

A category of their own

To solve this problem, we decided on the fly to create a new category: type revival.

Judges do have the power to move an entry from one category to another, if they think the face was entered in the wrong one. One year, in fact, the judges liked only one of the actual typefaces in a multi-weight, multi-style type family, so they decided to consider that face by itself as a single typeface. This year, some of the judges particularly liked individual characters in a couple of the entries, but not the whole typeface. It would be going too far, however, to extract only the characters you liked and judge them separately. All the constituent parts of a typeface have to work together.

With the new category, recognizing the specific nature of the entries that everyone recognized as revivals, the judges were willing to include two of them as winners.

Script rewrites

Then we started considering whether to include another of the entries, which was based on someone's handwriting, as a revival. Clearly, the design is based on an original — and the handwriting in this case was not the designer's but someone else's. Yet turning handwriting or calligraphy into type is no easy business; there are innumerable choices that have to be made. No one writes a single letter exactly the same way twice, so the designer has to choose which instance of the written letter will work best in a typeface. The relationships of the letters to each other will also vary in handwriting (especially in script, where the letters actually join). But in type, the exact same characters are going to be repeated over and over again.

One of the typeface entries that inspired the creation of a "revival" category: Menhart, by Alex W. White, based on a metal typeface by the Czech type designer Oldřich Menhart.

Turning handwriting into type takes a type designer's eye. The consensus was that this is essentially a process of design, not just imitation, and that it shouldn't be considered in the same way as a direct type revival.

The long tradition of typeface revivals

Creating a category won't solve all the problems, or simplify the questions. There are many more variations than came up in this particular type-design competition.

Many of the best-known fonts available to designers today are revivals — either of hot-metal typefaces from the 20th century or of foundry types from centuries before. Some of the 20th-century faces are themselves revivals — such as the various versions of Janson, which were based on the 17th-century metal types of Miklós Kis, and which in turn have been given photo and digital versions of varying utility.

When Robert Slimbach, for example, delved deep into the historical archives at the Plantin-Moretus Museum while researching the typefaces of Claude Garamond, for Adobe's attempt to make a definitive version of Garamond (released as Adobe Garamond), there is no question that he was working on a type revival. Yet he had to make choices along the way about which sizes to use as models, what tiny features would really be effective in a digital typeface, how to compensate for the lack of ink spread in offset printing, and so on. It's easier to be true to the designer's intentions if you have the original punches, rather than having to rely only on printed examples (as is the case with some early types, such as those cut by Griffo for Aldus Manutius around 1500); but even then, choices have to be made. And in the case of Adobe Garamond, what Slimbach was trying to do was not only revive Garamond's original fonts but create a family of typefaces in various weights — something that neither Claude Garamond nor anyone else had thought to do in the 16th century.

If the effort is simply — "simply"! — to render in digital form a typeface that was originally designed for a Linotype or Monotype typesetting machine, there is much less interpretation needed. But there is always some. Compare the digital versions of Centaur, for instance, or Bembo, with the hot-metal faces from Monotype used in so many books during the last 70 or 80 years. How much should the outlines of the letters be regularized for digital use? How idiosyncratically accurate should they be? Is it even possible, ever, to get exactly the same effect from a digital typeface as you'd get from the corresponding type set in metal?

Just as another example, consider the type family that Robert Slimbach created after Adobe Garamond, as another fruit of his researches: Minion. Although it was not a direct revival of any particular punchcutter's work, it was very much a Renaissance-style typeface. Yet it could only be considered an original design.

Gimme that old-time type design
Creativity is not at war with accuracy. But when it comes to making new typefaces based on old ones, the lines blur. I suppose the only true criterion for judging such work is the intent behind it. If it's an attempt to take credit for someone else's work, it should be condemned. If it's an attempt to render that work in a new medium, it should be judged for how well it does that.

There are those who argue that we should never try to revive older typefaces, that a type designer should always try to create something new. This is a minority opinion, but it's been cogently argued by some highly respected people. There isn't any question, however, that as type users — typographers — we have all benefited from many, many successful type revivals.

Sumner Stone, from the photo in the frontispiece of FONT.

Type traditions in a digital age

The catalog of an exhibition in England on the work of Sumner Stone and modern type design, bridges the gap between the quiet traditions of lettering and what we see on our computer screens.

[*July 20, 2001*]

The history of type on the computer might have developed entirely differently than it did. Instead of having the whole panoply of typographic possibilities quite literally at our fingertips, we might have been stuck with something limited and awkward. Luckily for us all, people who understood type and lettering were involved in the development of the desktop publishing revolution. Among the most influential was Sumner Stone, who was the focus of an exhibit at England's Ditchling Museum and its companion book, *Font*.

Sumner Stone is probably best known as the director of typography from 1984 to 1989 at Adobe Systems, where he led the way to make Adobe a leader in the design of digital type and the promulgation of digital typography. He designed the Stone super-family of typefaces (Stone Serif, Stone Sans, and Stone Informal), and his out-of-print book *On Stone* is — despite its concentration on one type designer's work — one of the best introductory books on type and how to use it.

In 2000, the Ditchling Museum, an institution in Sussex on the site of one of Eric Gill's would-be monastic typographic communities, put on an exhibition called "Font: Sumner Stone, Calligraphy and Type Design in a Digital Age"; the exhibition explored "the relationship between calligraphy, type and the new digital technology through the work of one of the world's greatest typographers: the American Sumner Stone." (This exhibition was the second part of a three-part series called "Lettering Today and Tomorrow." The first part, in 1999, was called "Handwriting: Everyone's Art"; the third, in 2001, was "The Flowing Line: The Influence of Japanese and Arabic Calligraphy in the West.")

In conjunction with the exhibition, the Ditchling Museum and the Edward Johnston Foundation published a small, pleasingly made book, also called *Font*, to document and supplement what was shown in Ditchling. The book contains several well-illustrated essays on type, technology, and the traditions of hand lettering; together, they provide an intelligent snapshot of how these influences, which now seem to go together so naturally, gave us the digital tools and the publishing environment that we now take for granted.

As the introduction by Ewan Clayton and Gerald Fleuss points out, the technology of the personal computer "was developed by computer scientists with no knowledge of lettering or typographic issues. Consequently in the early eighties there was a real danger that the knowledge of the lettering community would be ignored." But the San Francisco Bay Area — ground zero in technical development — "already had a flourishing tradition of fine press printing and a lively calligraphic community. Rather than stand its distance this community got involved. With hindsight this was one of the crucial moments in the evolution of the Roman alphabet and its usage, as important as those early years of the fifteenth century in Florence when a handful of humanist scholars developed the new conventions in manuscript production that would combine with the arrival of print and determine the course of that technology."

Basalt: a roman sans serif

Stone's lead-off article in this book tells about the process of developing a new typeface, Basalt, which started out as a fantasy of creating a higher-quality model for handwriting in elementary schools and became an attempt to create "a classical Roman sans serif." Our well-known serif letterforms have a clear line of descent, from the inscriptions on the Trajan column in Rome and other classical monuments, but sans-serif forms have what Stone calls a "broken history." "Unlike serifed forms," he says, "where the inscribed lettering of Imperial Rome has served as a model during the Renaissance and into modern times, there is no canonical sans serif letter. The problem of creating one is similar to the problem faced by Virgil in creating a mythological history for Rome."

Stone's classical sans serif "would be a fiction, like the Aeneid. In my fantasy, Basalt would be the sans serif companion to the most formal Roman inscriptional forms, like those used on the tomb of Cecilia Metalla. If Romans had used computers, it would have been there on every screen, Metalla and Basalt."

One of Stone's early sketches of Basalt, from FONT.

Basalt isn't entirely conceived as a fantasy; it has a real-world purpose, too. Stone intended Basalt to be useful as a typeface for signage, and indeed its first public use is for signage in the libraries at Stanford University.

"The signs I am fascinated by," says Stone, "are those in which text typography is required, such as street signs, directional signs, informational signs, memorials, inscriptions, dedications. These are all examples of public lettering."

As he points out, "real things are at stake" when you're dealing with signage: "like finding your way or becoming lost." Making signs that real people will use is not an intellectual exercise. "Examples of one of my favorite signage systems can still be found in California's Sierra Nevada mountains, where surviving a winter is a significant accomplishment for a sign. They were made by cutting letters out of steel plate with a torch."

```
ABCDEFGHIJKLM
NOPQRSTUVWXYZ
ABCDEFGHIJKLM
NOPQRSTUVWXYZ
1234567890
```

```
ABCDEFGHIJKLM
NOPQRSTUVWXYZ
ABCDEFGHIJKLM
NOPQRSTUVWXYZ
1234567890
```

Stone created two versions of
Basalt — the normal version
(top) and a slightly narrower
version (bottom).

One of the considerations that Stone kept in mind when designing Basalt was the question of size, or scale. "As you approach a sign, you first see it at some distance, and then you may move closer. Usually, it is desirable to be able to read the sign from as far away as possible as well as when you are close to it." So the letters have to work both small — or apparently small, when viewed from far away — and large. "The further away the viewer is, the smaller the letters appear. A letter which is four inches tall appears to the reader to be only a 6 pt character when viewed from the appropriate distance, so in some respects the problem is similar to designing type which is to be used exclusively at small sizes, as in the telephone book or classified advertisements in the newspaper." But signage type, unlike the type in a telephone book, also has to work at large size when seen up close. At large size, "ugly and awkward letters can be just as distracting as those which are too beautiful or quirky."

Stone's Basalt is a typeface all in caps, like the inscriptions that inspired it. But Stone discovered that the basic letterforms he was working with would also work when they were slightly condensed, without losing any of their legibility or usefulness. So he created a narrower version and put it into the lowercase position in the digital font. The narrower alphabet "can be used along with the wider forms without looking cramped or drawing attention to itself," according to Stone.

Space, geometry, and cyberspace

Sumner Stone's "Basalt" is only one of the essays contained in this book, though it's certainly the central one. Of the other three essays, the most useful is "Watch this Space," by John Dreyfus. Dreyfus succeeded Stanley Morison as typographical advisor to the Monotype Corporation in England, which put him at the center of the typographic world of the mid-twentieth century. He has written voluminously (a collection of his writing,

Into Print, unfortunately priced beyond the means of most type aficionados, was published in 1995 by David Godine), and his short essay here touches on any number of important questions about how type works and how to practice the art of lettering. Perhaps the most provocative is one posed by a music teacher attended by the theater director Peter Brook: "Why is rhythm the common factor in all arts?" Dreyfus says, "in typography and lettering, I reckon that rhythm comes from the finely adjusted relationships between the letters in our alphabet which have developed through several millennia of use." His conclusion (after all, the essay is called "Watch this Space") is: "If the subtle balances which exist between the shapes and the voids of our Roman alphabet are matched by harmonious spacing between words and lines…, then a rhythm will be achieved which can lift typography and lettering to the level of an art."

The other two essays, "Slouching toward Cyberspace" by David Levy and "The Geometry of Roman Lettering" by Tom Perkins, are interesting but not on the same lively level as Stone's and Dreyfus's offerings. The Perkins essay is copiously illustrated, to show the relations between the Golden Rectangle and a number of other classic geometrical forms and the letterforms on the ancient Roman formal inscriptions such as the Trajan column. I tend to find this kind of esoteric geometry a little tenuous, drawing connections where maybe none existed; but it's perfectly possible that it was the ancient Roman inscriptional artists who got a little carried away, not Tom Perkins.

Design in the hand

Font is a short book, just 64 pages, but as a paperback in landscape format, with dimensions of 9 inches high by just over 9½ inches wide, it's a floppy little volume. It's elegantly designed, using another of Sumner Stone's text typefaces, Cycles Eleven. Yet there are curiosities in both

Cover of the book FONT.

its design and its execution. Is a classic medieval arrangement of the text block, with a huge bottom margin, wide outer margin, and proportionally decreasing top and inner margins, really appropriate to a two-column arrangement of text in a landscape format? There may be medieval antecedents, but it seems a little weird today. And the proofreading of the typeset text could have been better; among other things, we find different treatments of fractions in different paragraphs.

Nonetheless, it's basically a well-conceived book, and one that feels good in the hands as you read it. It is certainly worth seeking out and acquiring.

The next Sabon

Jean François Porchez updates Jan Tschichold's typeface Sabon, going back to Tschichold's sources and eliminating the compromises required by hot-metal technology.
[*March 7, 2003*]

EVER SINCE its introduction in 1967, Sabon has been one of the most useful of text typefaces. It is frequently used in books, because it's classic in form but sturdy and practical in execution. It reads well. Now Linotype Library, as part of its program of refining the digital forms of older typefaces and issuing updated versions, has commissioned Jean François Porchez to create a new Sabon: Sabon Next. How do the two compare?

Three in one
Sabon has an unusual history. It was commissioned by a consortium of the German printing industry, who wanted a new text typeface that would work equally well on both Linotype and Monotype machines (the two dominant hot-metal typesetting systems) and as hand-set type (to be issued by the Stempel foundry). The new typeface was to look for its roots and inspiration to the 16th-century types of the French typecutter Claude Garamond, but to be a practical modern-day text face. They asked Jan Tschichold to design it.

Tschichold was a superb typographer. A one-time radical modernist who fled from Nazi Germany to Switzerland, he eventually turned his practice 180 degrees and became an outspoken advocate of classical typography. He was certainly one of the finest book designers of the 20th century — not just of "beautiful books" for connoisseurs but also of mass-market paperbacks like those published by Penguin (he redesigned the whole line and set new standards for it after the Second World War).

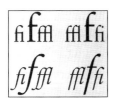

Traditional long f forms (left) and the compact f forms used in the original design of Sabon.

Tschichold designed very few typefaces, but Sabon was his masterwork; it has become a modern classic.

Hemmed in

The constraints that Tschichold had to work within, in designing Sabon, didn't bother him (it was "no effort at all," he claimed, to make it work with three different typesetting systems), but they certainly influenced the shape of the type. First of all, he had to fit all of the letters into the Monotype machine's 18-unit width system; every letter had to be an even number of units wide. That wasn't too hard. For handset foundry type, he had to take into account the "German standard baseline," which was based on the proportions of blackletter fonts and left very little space for descenders. Tschichold managed to turn the short descenders into a virtue, so that they looked natural and compact.

The most awkward restrictions came from the Linotype.

On a Linotype machine, the roman and italic were generally "duplexed" — that is, contained on the same matrix — which meant that they had to be the same width. But italic is traditionally narrower than the roman it accompanies. The Linotype also can't kern, which is why the lowercase italic *f* in some Linotype faces seems to be awkwardly straightening itself up and tucking its extenders in, to avoid overlapping the letters on either side. Tschichold finessed the latter problem by creating an italic *f* with a straight tail, rather than the long curving tail that was common. And in designing his italic for Sabon, he made an open, readable italic that didn't look as though it had been stretched to fit.

He actually got to create a narrower italic for the display sizes, since the Monotype and Linotype versions were designed for setting text at 12pt and under; larger sizes would be set by hand, using the Stempel foundry type. As Jean François Porchez puts it, "The second version of Sabon was designed by Tschichold for Stempel metal handsetting, for sizes of 14 pt and over, and it seems closer to a pure interpretation of Garamond without all the constraints described above. Sadly, when Linotype and Monotype adapted the design to their photocomposition systems, they did not follow the Stempel version." In photo and later digital versions of Sabon, some of the features that Tschichold created to meet the technical requirements and to work at text sizes can look a little clunky when blown up large. The unusually round lowercase italic *o* is one that sticks out.

A comparison of the previous digital version of Sabon Italic (top) and the new italic of Sabon Next (bottom).

Hamburgefonts
Hamburgefonts

Old & improved

When Porchez set out to reinterpret Sabon, he wanted to do it without the compromises that Tschichold had had to make. He wanted to go back to the original typefaces that Tschichold had used as his models, and make something that was faithful both to the typeface that Tschichold designed and to the original. In doing this, he discovered another source. Tschichold had always said that he took his inspiration from the 1592 Egenolff-Berner type specimen sheet, which shows several sizes of Garamond's roman paired with Robert Granjon's italics; Porchez is convinced that Tschichold was also looking at another specimen, showing the roman types cut by Guillaume II Le Bé, whose father had bought most of Garamond's punches and matrices after he died. So Porchez looked back to both specimens as he worked on his new digital version.

The new typeface, Sabon Next, is in some ways more a revival of Garamond (and Le Bé) than of Sabon—if such a fine distinction can be made. It's interesting to compare Sabon Next with Adobe Garamond, Robert Slimbach's ambitious revival for which he researched Garamond's original punches in the Plantin-Moretus Museum in Antwerp. The two digital typefaces are different interpretations of the same sources. It's especially easy to see the resemblance in the italics, but even the romans have a similar color. Sabon Next has an advantage over Adobe Garamond, however: Sabon Next includes an extra version of the roman and italic that have been beefed up a bit for use at small sizes. (Curiously, Linotype calls these Regular and the finer version Display, even though they recommend using the Display version for sizes of 11pt and larger. Usually "display" refers to non-text sizes—at least 18pt. I would probably use Regular for any serious text work, and not switch to Display until 14pt or larger.) Sabon Next also includes something that the old Sabon never did: a complete range of heavier weights. Tschichold did design a bold (though no bold italic), but Porchez has added not only a bold (with italic) but a demi, an extra bold, and a black.

The Linotype specimen booklet for Sabon Next shows the subtle differences between the Display and Regular versions, intended for different sizes of text.

The objective was to provide two isually two different text sizes on a or example). Just compare this paragraph composed in Regular to the rest of the text in Display. er in terms of elements to fit the esigned more weights, up to Black.

Sabon Next has some notable differences from Tschichold's Sabon in the details. In the original Sabon, for instance, the cap-height (lining) zero is an ellipse with thicker sides and thinner top and bottom; the old-style (lowercase) zero is a perfect circle, with no modulation at all to its stroke. That perfect circle is used in many old-style typefaces, and it has a long history, but it has always disturbed me. Yes, it makes it impossible to mistake the zero for an **o**, but it doesn't fit with the modulated strokes of the other numerals. For Sabon Next, Porchez has chosen to echo the unusual arrangement used in Stempel Garamond (widely regarded as the most faithful revival of Garamond's types, at least until recently): a zero with the thickness at the top and bottom rather than the sides. He uses this in both the cap-height zero and the lowercase zero. As in Stempel Garamond, it stands out — but it looks odd. I'm not sure where this style came from; there are no Arabic numerals at all on the Egenolff-Berner specimen sheet.

The lowercase roman **a** and **s** are narrower in Sabon Next; Porchez felt strongly that the unusually wide **a** and **s** in Sabon were a mistake, occasioned by the limitations of the Monotype and Linotype systems. This may be the case, but in use those wide **a**'s and **s**'s give Sabon part of its character — part of what makes it something more than just another Garamond revival. Certainly the narrower **a** and **s** give a different look and feel to a line of text in Sabon Next — as do the roman **f** with a longer top curve, the italic *f* with its curling tail, and, on a subtler level, the italic *p* with a normal serif on the bottom of the descender, rather than the righthand-only serif that Tschichold used (again to avoid kerning problems). (Some of these forms have been preserved as alternates in the new fonts.)

The accents — acute, grave, and circumflex — are much taller and more vertical than in Sabon; these follow Garamond's originals closely, and certainly look well in French.

On the shoulders of giants
On the whole, Sabon Next is more elegant than Sabon, though it doesn't seem to have quite the robustness that characterizes the Tschichold version.

The very first use of the new Sabon Next was in a commemorative booklet about the Prix Charles Peignot, designed by Jean François Porchez and published by ATypI for its 2002 conference.

A new version of a typeface is always a new typeface, no matter how closely it hews to the original design. As such, it should be judged on its own terms. Sabon Next is clearly a useful addition to our typographic repertoire. Producing it was a major undertaking, and each of the myriad decisions about the exact form of a letter or the angle of a curve was made deliberately — just as those decisions were made almost 40 years ago by Jan Tschichold, working within the constraints of the technology of his time. I'm looking forward to getting my hands on the new Sabon Next and giving it a practical workout; as a book designer, I've used Sabon many times, and I'm curious to see whether Sabon Next seems a good replacement — or something different and new, with its own style and its own uses.

After completing the project, Jean François Porchez said, "I like to imagine what Jan Tschichold, and by extension Claude Garamond and Guillaume Le Bé, would think about this revival — I dream that they would probably follow similar design decisions faced with today's less limited technical possibilities. Sabon Next was a really passionate project for me, and a real pleasure to stand on the shoulders of such giants. I hope that Sabon will now be appreciated not only because it is a Tschichold design — free from any criticism of how Linotype/Monotype limitations restricted Tschichold's first ideas — but also for the real quality of a good text face which has been renourished by the two sides of its roots."

DTL Fleischmann *was drawn by Erhard Kaiser, who based the design on the 18th-century type of Johann Michael Fleischmann.*

Dutch Type Library

The Dutch Type Library is less well known in North America than it deserves to be.

[*April 17, 2003*]

THE DUTCH TYPE LIBRARY (DTL), despite its official-sounding name, is not the most widely known source of new Dutch type designs, nor do all of the fonts it sells come from the hands of Dutch designers. But it represents a useful collection of well-thought-out typeface families that are not as well known in North America as they ought to be.

Old type in new bottles

The foundry is the brainchild of Frank E. Blokland, and it's based in 's-Hertogenbosch. (Don't be confused by the coincidental resemblance of Blokland's name to the names of his compatriots, Erik van Blokland and Petr van Blokland; Erik and Petr are brothers, but Frank is unrelated to them, although they are all type designers and they all studied at the same school.) The heart of the DTL collection is revivals of typefaces from the history of Dutch type design. Dutch punchcutters and type founders dominated European printing in the 17th century, and the Netherlands has been a source of typographic creativity in the 20th and 21st. One of the Dutch Type Library's releases, several years ago, was DTL Vanden-Keere, a revival of the elegant typefaces created in the 16th century — well before the supposed heyday of Dutch punchcutting — by Hendrik van den Keere (whose types have also, coincidentally, served as the basis of an unrelated family of digital newspaper fonts). A 20th-century Dutch type designer, Jan van Krimpen, was arguably the first to design a sans-serif type family as a deliberate companion to a serif family; DTL has continued and extended that tradition by bringing out a digital version of Van

Krimpen's neglected Haarlemmer typeface and then creating a new Haarlemmer Sans to go with it.

All of the DTL typefaces are text families, or extended families that include both text and display versions, and some of them include an almost bewildering variety of weights, styles, and variations. Indeed, the only serious fault of the Dutch Type Library's offerings may be that it's hard to get an overview of all the typefaces and their variations, either from catalogs or from the company's web site. On the other hand, as I have mentioned before, DTL has produced some very fine type specimens for individual type families; I've learned to look in my goody bag at ATypI conferences to see what DTL may have come out with this time.

aindgos*aindgosz*

One of those type specimens, a couple of years ago, was a 32-page booklet showcasing DTL Fleischmann, a revival of the idiosyncratic Baroque typefaces cut by Johann Michael Fleischmann in the 18th century. (His name is also sometimes spelled Joan Michael Fleischman.) The digital DTL Fleischmann, which has a robust weight to the regular text face and some very distinctive, attention-getting details in some of the letters, was created by Erhard Kaiser, a German type designer who worked for Typoart in Leipzig before the reunification of Germany. (Perhaps because the designer is German, the text of the Fleischmann specimen is entirely in German, rather than in DTL's native Dutch or in the most common international language of typography these days, English. It makes me wish I could read more German.)

More recently, Kaiser has completed an entirely different kind of typeface family, a new sans serif called DTL Prokyon, which owes very little to any earlier typeface. This too merits a well-produced 32-page specimen book (again, *auf Deutsch*) that shows off the weights and styles, and the design details and unusual touches, quite thoroughly. Prokyon is largely monoweight, like most sans serifs, and has fairly classical proportions; its most noticeable trait is its simplification of the forms of some common letters: particularly lowercase **a**, **m**, **n**, and **r**. Kaiser says that his aim was "Formreduktion" or simplification of the letter shapes, starting with the **m** and **n**. This simplification, which almost eliminates the curves of those two letters, works surprisingly well in text. Even the odd form of the lowercase **g**, in which a one-storey design includes a little "ear" that is simply a continuation of the curved stroke beyond the stem, doesn't draw too much attention to itself in a block of text; and it certainly makes the typeface easy to identify.

Kaiser also developed DTL *Prokyon, a sans-serif typeface that's not a revival of an earlier face but completely new.*

Klassische Proportionen und moderne Formen

Klassische Proportionen und moderne Formen

Klassische Proportionen und moderne Formen

Like many DTL typefaces, Prokyon includes three different kinds of numerals: uppercase or lining numerals (which match the cap height), lowercase or old-style numerals (which match the x-height and have asenders and descenders), and small-caps numerals (which match the small-cap height, a little taller than the x-height, and have very slight ascenders and descenders). There are also superior and inferior numerals, and fractions. All four weights include small caps, in both the roman and the italic.

In use, at least judging by the specimen, DTL Prokyon looks clean and modern, while having enough variety to be readable. DTL (or perhaps Erhard Kaiser) describes it as having "classical proportions and modern forms."

Es waren zwei
Neuerungen, die die
Designer von den
Künstlern der frühen
Avantgarde aufgrif-
fen, zwei Themen,
die heute noch von
Es waren zwei Neuerungen, die die Designer
großer BEDEUTUNG
von den Künstlern der frühen Avantgarde auf-
sind: RAUM und
griffen, zwei Themen, die heute noch von großer
BEWEGUNG.
Bedeutung sind: RAUM UND BEWEGUNG.

A small clan of large families

The two different type designs by Erhard Kaiser neatly
represent the opposite ends of the DTL design spectrum,
from Baroque revival to streamlined modern. Other
noteworthy typefaces include Gerard Unger's DTL Argo
and DTL Paradox, Michael Harvey's DTL Unico, Elmo
van Slingerland's DTL Dorian, and DTL Nobel, a revival
by Andrea Fuchs and Fred Smeijers of the 1930 geometric sans by S. H. de Roos.

DTL also manufactures one of the current crop of
font-developers' tools, DTL Fontmaster — but that's
another subject.

If the Dutch Type Library hasn't become as well
known in the North American market as you might
think, one reason is that the fonts have only been available directly from DTL — and for a long time the website
was only in Dutch. It might also be because DTL fonts are
relatively expensive, by the current depressed standards
of font pricing: a flat price of €100 per single font (€125
to combine the old-style-figure and lining-figure versions
of the same font), with a 10% discount when you buy the
whole family. Not exactly mass-market pricing, but it
may assure a fairer return to the typeface designers for
their work. And all of the DTL typefaces look like they'd
be workhorses that you would use again and again, not
just one-time novelties.

The Enschedé Type Foundry

The tradition of one of Europe's oldest type foundries is carried on in a new form by the Enschedé Font Foundry.
[*August 9, 2003*]

THE ENSCHEDÉ FONT FOUNDRY (TEFF) is the digital successor to one of the great historical type foundries of Europe. Joh. Enschedé en Zonen, founded in 1703, produced a host of noteworthy typefaces for hand-setting and letterpress printing over the course of more than two and a half centuries, and its type-specimen books are rare compendiums of the development of metal type. TEFF today offers just five font families (so far, at least), but they all bring a deep knowledge of historical type founding and design to the creation of contemporary digital fonts, intended for current technology and uses.

A new branch from old roots
Joh. Enschedé en Zonen was founded in 1703, in the city of Haarlem in the Netherlands. It began as a printery, and it is still active as one of the most important printers in the Netherlands, printing the country's stamps and banknotes among other things. Enschedé began manufacturing type in 1743, after buying an existing type foundry, and over the course of more than two centuries, type founding was one of the most important parts of Enschedé's business. Many of the most respected type designers, from Joan Michael Fleischman in the 18th century to Jan van Krimpen in the 20th, worked for Enschedé. But Enschedé, like so many of the old-line type manufacturers, was severely affected by the changing technologies and business models of the font business, and in 1990 the type-foundry was moved out of its historic buildings, and effectively ceased to be a business.

The Enschedé Font Foundry was established in 1991 by Peter Matthias Noordzij, to carry on the Enschedé tradition in a new form. Rather than reviving old metal typefaces, he began by releasing a PostScript version of Trinité, which had been designed just a decade earlier (for Enschedé's 275th anniversary) by Bram de Does as a phototype face. All the releases since then have been original, although one, Fred Smeijers's Renard, draws its inspiration from types cut in the 16th century by the early Dutch punchcutter Hendrik van den Keere.

Variations on a theme

The model followed by Noordzij is clearly one of doing a few things but doing them very well. Each of the five TEFF type families comprises more than the usual selection of weights and variations. Trinité, for instance, was designed as an elegant old-style text face but in three different versions, identical except for the length of the ascenders and descenders (collectively, "extenders"); there's a version with short extenders, for use where the lines have to be set very tight; a version with very long extenders, for fancy setting on a spacious page; and an in-between version for everyday use. All three versions are available as part of TEFF's digital version of Trinité, along with a swash version of the long-extender italic.

The many variations of
Bram de Does's Trinité, with
its three lengths of ascenders
and descenders.

Trinité also comes in both normal ("wide") and condensed widths, in its roman style; the italic is narrow and designed to work with either of them.

Even more complex is Lexicon, also designed by Bram de Does (in 1992), which has only two lengths of extenders but comes in no fewer than six subtly graded weights. It is an elegant typeface, very much in the Dutch old-style tradition, but it was designed to stand up to laser printing and use at very small sizes; it has been used in everything from office memoes to one of the biggest Dutch dictionaries.

Lexicon comes with three different kinds of numerals: old-style (lowercase) figures with varying widths, "tabular" old-style figures (all the same width, so they'll line up when set in columns), and tabular lining (uppercase) figures. It also has small capitals for all the weights (and italic small caps, too — a very useful addition). Interestingly, TEFF puts tabular old-style figures in the small-caps font; I would have expected the non-tabular old-style figures instead.

Renard is a serif face designed by Fred Smeijers, whose best-known typeface is FF Quadraat; Smeijers is also the author of *Counterpunch*, a book that spans the technological gap between punchcutting and digital type design. Although Renard is based on a display-size type that Hendrik van den Keere cut in 1570, it is meant to be a text face. As Smeijers says, "Van den Keere's typeface was cut in a large size for display setting: for use in choirbooks for example. Such a book would be placed in front of the choir, so it had to be legible for all the singers in poor lighting conditions." So although the typeface was quite large, it was meant to be seen at a distance — effectively at text sizes. "To achieve legibility the typeface is rather condensed, with a large x-height and dark overall colour. Van den Keere never cut a complete italic, so Renard's italic is a new design, made in the spirit of the period."

The three subtly different weights of Fred Smeijers's Renard, with some of the original punches of the 16th-century types it was inspired by.

Collis, designed by Christoph Noordzij (Matthias's brother) in 1993, is aptly described as "a typical 'The Hague-style' typeface with a certain elegance." The

Christoph Noordzij's "Hague-style" typeface Collis.

design school in the Hague, where Matthias and Christoph's father Gerrit taught for many years, is the source of an amazing number of contemporary Dutch type designers, and it's easy to see a connection among them, in both their knowledge of the Dutch type-design tradition and their attention to letterforms and how letters get made. Collis is meant to work at both small sizes and display sizes; its distribution of weight and its low contrast between thick and thin strokes make it useful for high-impact text use, in posters, brochures, and ads. It comes in only one weight, in roman and italic, but it has the same variety of numerals as Lexicon, and it has an oddity of its own: a "Bible" version, where the capital letters with accents are slightly smaller than normal, so the accents don't extend up above the cap height and you can set the space between lines very tight. (I'm not convinced that this is a good idea, but Collis gives you the option.)

The family theme is carried through in the last of the five TEFF typefaces, Ruse, which is designed by Gerrit Noordzij. It is a modern face (that is, "modern" in the typographic sense: high contrast, vertical stress, mostly unbracketed serifs), reminiscent a little bit of the text sizes of the early-19th-century classic Walbaum. But Ruse is based on Gerrit Noordzij's handwriting, and on his ideas about how the "ductus" of writing influences the design of type: "I transferred the rhythm of the written word image into this typeface: the emphasis lies on the balance between the white shapes that keep the black shapes in place. The appearance of the typeface is casual, but what's casual for me doesn't necessarily have to be for other people. Let's say that I excluded any striking peculiarities." Ruse has the largest number of weights of any TEFF typeface — eleven — with the increase in weight built up by increasing the contrast between thick and thin strokes. The heaviest weight is hard to imagine using very often, but the variations remind me of the changing appearance of Robert Slimbach's Kepler, which used multiple-master technology to span a wide range of weights in a similarly lively, calligraphic modern face. Ruse too has the common TEFF arrangement of old-style and lining figures.

RUSE 1000 – 2100

A&aaaaaaaaaaa&A
aaaaaaaaaa

Value for money

The Enschedé Font Foundry charges a good deal more than the going rate for its fonts. The TEFF type families offer good value, but they're not casual purchases; they're meant to be workhorses that will be useful in many kinds of jobs over a long period of time. In pricing its fonts this way, TEFF is joining several other manufacturers of high-quality fonts in trying to counter the tendency to make type a commodity that's practically given away for nothing. This is an effort that seems to have originated in the Netherlands; others taking the same approach include the Dutch Type Library, and designer Gerard Unger with his newspaper face Gulliver. It seems a reasonable way to compensate type designers for some of the long hours and high skill required to make a really good, versatile typeface.

Mr. Jefferson's typeface

Matthew Carter's Monticello is a revival of the typeface used to print Thomas Jefferson's complete papers.

[*August 22, 2003*]

THOMAS JEFFERSON wasn't a typographer, but he took an interest in every kind of technology and scientific knowledge in his time, and he encouraged the development of home-grown American industry to promote the growth and independence of the new nation. When Archibald Binny and James Ronaldson, immigrants from Scotland who had established a type foundry in Philadelphia, asked the former president for his help in obtaining antimony (used in casting metal type) when their existing supply was interrupted by an international trade dispute, Jefferson helped them find a new source in France. And in later years, Jefferson expressed his admiration for the types of Binny & Ronaldson, which by the 1820s had become the most commonly used types in the United States.

Binny & Ronaldson was one of the first type foundries in the United States, established in Philadelphia in 1796.

Binny & Ronaldson

Graphic tastes change, however, and Binny & Ronaldson's "Pica Roman No. 1" was eclipsed by newer types in the middle of the 19th century. When it was revived in 1892, under the name "Oxford," by the American Type Founders Company (a grand consortium of most of the U.S. type foundries, formed in reaction to the competition of the newly invented typesetting machines), the typeface became a favorite of several of the foremost American typographers and book designers, including Bruce Rogers and Daniel Berkeley Updike. Updike used it as the text type for his monumental two-volume study of the history of type, *Printing Types: Their History, Forms,*

The centerpiece of a broadside prepared to show the original Oxford foundry type, the hot-metal Linotype Monticello, and the new digital Monticello together.

and Use (which had the secondary subtitle *A Study in Survivals*), where he described Oxford as a "transitional" design between the old-fashioned style of old face (such as Caslon) and the crisper but less readable "modern" style derived from the work of Bodoni and Didot. He praised Oxford very simply but tellingly: "I have used it for this book. It seems to me a type of real distinction."

More than a hundred years after Jefferson admired the typeface that came to be called Oxford, Princeton University Press proposed to publish Jefferson's complete papers, and C. H. Griffith of Mergenthaler Linotype suggested that it should be done in "a historically appropriate typeface, one with which Jefferson was intimately familiar and which he expressly admired" (according to the broadside that accompanies the new digital adaptation). With the help of P. J. Conkwright, book designer at Princeton, Griffith worked on developing a machine version of Oxford that could be used on the Linotype. "Together they strove to preserve the spirit and style of the original design while moving it to a radically different technology. It would take them six years to complete the roman, italic, and small-capital fonts in seven sizes (7, 8, 9, 10, 11, 12, and 14 points), each of which required a separate cutting." They named the new Linotype version "Monticello," in honor of Jefferson.

A resetting in digital Monticello of an illustration in metal of which C. H. Griffith wrote, "These enlarged letters show the rather lively variation in serif treatment and bracketing which contribute to the inherent readability of Monticello."

But the Linotype, too, eventually became old technology, supplanted by the new. The Press's printing program used Monticello in hot metal for many years, but by the

Monticello
Monticello
Monticello

The development of digital Monticello: top, the unedited data supplied to Matthew Carter by Linotype; middle, a PostScript font converted from the Linotron 202 data, with tiny straight lines but no curves; bottom, the new digital Monticello.

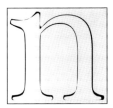

The Linotype outline character with the new digital version superimposed on top of it. "This shows," Carter says, "that the weight was not added by dipping the too-light version in chocolate, but by selectively putting more on the serifs than on the upright strokes."

1980s they had to enter the era of digital typesetting, and they had to somehow adapt Monticello. Mergenthaler supplied a digital version that would work on the Linotron 202 digital typesetter, but there were many compromises involved, and with each new turn the typesetting technology took, the makeshift nature of this first digital adaptation of Monticello became more and more apparent. Finally, in 2002, Princeton University Press turned to Matthew Carter and commissioned him to create a new digital Monticello that could take advantage of modern typesetting systems.

Going back to roots

A digital font does not need to make some of the compromises that were necessary in adapting a design to the Linotype machine. It was no longer necessary for the italic alphabet and the roman to have exactly the same width (in most type families, the italic looks most natural when it's a bit narrower than the roman), and there was no need to avoid overhanging kerns like the projecting ends of the italic *f*. While Carter's brief was to adapt Linotype Monticello to PostScript, he also looked back to the original Binny & Ronaldson types and brought back some of the features that had been lost in the interim.

One feature that had been added in the interim has been kept as an option in the new typeface. Although Oxford had, in keeping with the prevailing style when it was first cast, possessed only lining figures (uppercase figures, all of them the same height, though in this case not as high as the capital letters), when Linotype was developing a photo version of Monticello in 1973, they had added old-style (lowercase) figures as well. The new digital Monticello offers two versions of both the roman and the italic fonts: one with lining figures, one with old-style figures. (Matthew Carter told me that in the hot-metal version of Monticello, the small caps font that Linotype shipped with the typeface was in fact taken

*A sample of digital Monti-
cello used in text on the
broadside prepared by Princeton University Press.*

from Baskerville, and that before the advent of old-style
figures for Monticello, printers had to take them from
other fonts; the old-style figures from Caledonia worked
surprisingly well.)

Since the digital Monticello is intended primarily
for book work, it has to appear strong and dark at small
sizes. It has none of the spindliness that sometimes
appears in digital (and photo) adaptations of metal typefaces. Compared to the 12pt Linotype Monticello, digital
Monticello's characters are a bit wider, more like the
proportions in the smaller sizes of the metal type. The fit
of the letters seems a little bit tighter, especially at small
sizes (though in digital typesetting the spacing can be varied easily enough, for good or ill). While it's fascinating
to pore over the broadside prepared by Charles Creesy of
the Princeton University Press and compare the settings
of Oxford, Linotype Monticello, and digital Monticello
at various sizes, what counts to most of us is whether the
new version works. It does. It's a comfortably readable
face in a style that now looks old but familiar to us, and
it should lend itself quite well to book typography. I can
easily imagine Monticello, in its new form, becoming a
very popular book face once again.

In use today

When Matthew Carter gave a talk last winter to the
American Printing History Association, at the Grolier
Club in New York City, about the creation of digital
Monticello, APHA vice president Paul Romaine distributed as a keepsake a little sample that brought the typeface full circle. It was a single sheet, folded into a four-
page booklet, which reprinted a short letter that James
Ronaldson wrote to Thomas Jefferson in July 1822, and
Jefferson's even shorter but cordial reply. Ronaldson had
sent Jefferson a specimen of his company's latest printing types, and had bragged a little (justifiably) about how
he and Binny had helped establish type-founding in the

A LETTER OF
THOMAS JEFFERSON
TO
JAMES RONALDSON

On Printing Type &
Human Progress

The cover of a keepsake
printed for the American
Printing History Association
to celebrate the launch of
digital Monticello.

United States ("there are now in the US six letter foundries, and several Stereo ones, with the probability there will be more…"). Jefferson thanked him and observed, "Altho' increasing debility warns me that it cannot be long before the transactions of the world will close upon me, yet I feel ardent wishes for the continued progress of science and the arts, and the consequent advancement of the happiness of man. When I look back to Bell's edition of Blackstone (about 1773) and compare his with your types, and by the progress of the last half century estimate that of the centuries to come[,] I am cheared with the prospects of improvement in the human condition, which altho not infinite are certainly indefinite." The keepsake was set in digital Monticello but printed by plates on a letterpress by Kallemeyn Press — a fine melding of technologies from different eras.

The first use of Monticello in a book was in Volume 31 of the Jefferson Papers, published in early 2004. The digital fonts are available from Linotype Library, or directly from Carter & Cone Type Inc.

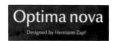

Optima nova

Hermann Zapf's classic typeface Optima, redesigned and updated by Zapf and Akira Kobayashi.

[*October 30, 2003*]

LINOTYPE HAS ISSUED a new version of Optima, designed by Hermann Zapf and Linotype's typographic director, Akira Kobayashi, and built from the ground up for digital typesetting. Most of the changes to this much-loved typeface are subtle; some are startling.

Optima was originally designed by Zapf more than fifty years ago; he made drawings of the face in 1952, though it wasn't released until 1958. It was cut in metal by the punchcutter August Rosenberger at the Stempel type foundry in Germany, and also turned into Linotype matrices for hot-metal typesetting. The new typeface was a departure from most type designs before it, since the letters had no serifs yet they were based on the classic forms of roman letters, and their serif-less strokes swelled slightly toward each end. This subtle curve to the "straight" strokes gave Optima a monumental elegance at large sizes, and made it work surprisingly well as a text face.

Optima has been adapted many times to photo and digital technologies, and it still remains a very popular typeface, but none of these translations has quite captured the beauty and the plain practicality of the original metal type. Trying to use Optima for text, in the age of digital typesetting, has been an exercise in wishful thinking—wishing that the digital version of the face were not quite so sparkly and light. At display sizes, some of the digital versions worked fine; but in text, none really did. If you've ever seen Hermann Zapf's little book *About Alphabets*, which is typeset in the original metal version of Optima, you can see how agreeable Optima can be for

A comparison of the original metal version of Optima (top) with the new Optima nova (bottom).

A sample of the current digital version of Optima (this is the Adobe font, licensed from Linotype).

A sample of the new Optima nova.

text; but this is an effect I've tried and failed many times to reproduce using digital versions.

Old & improved

Optima nova is part of Linotype's program of revisiting their best-selling typefaces and updating them for current technology. It's a debatable idea — should older typefaces be "updated," or should we leave them alone and design new faces for new uses? This question is a little like the perennial debate over "reviving" typefaces from centuries past, although in this case the typefaces are much more recent. In any case, Linotype's program has produced some interesting, and potentially useful, innovations.

Akira Kobayashi, a fine type designer in his own right, worked directly with Hermann Zapf in doing the new version of Optima. At the 2003 ATypI conference in Vancouver, Kobayashi described their process — Zapf sitting next to him, sketching out ideas, as Kobayashi worked with the outlines on the screen — and it was with evident pride and pleasure that Kobayashi told us how after a certain point, Zapf stopped sketching and simply made verbal suggestions — "Make this one better." Collaboration at its best.

The new Optima (for some reason Linotype likes to lowercase the word "nova") is much like the old, but beefed up a bit. Its thin strokes are a little thicker, which makes it work better in text. In fact, its "color" on the page comes much closer to that of the original metal version than any of the earlier photo/digital versions did.

In the basic roman style of Optima nova, there is only one noticeable change, but it calls attention to itself. The ends of the strokes in the letters **a**, **c**, and **s** flair much more dramatically than they ever did in the older Optima — so much so that these letters almost look as though they have serifs. It may be that the idea was that these semi-serifs would strengthen how the ends of the strokes look at text sizes, but at any larger size they make the new typeface look somehow busier than the old. It's a subtle difference, but it's disturbing if you're used to the under-stated elegance of Optima's letterforms.

Text set in the original hot-metal Optima (right) and in Optima nova (left).

Linotype typesetting machines. Unfortunal
no real italic was manufactured, only an ok
version of the roman.

The basic idea of Optima was to develop a
typeface between a sans serif like the Futur
a classical Roman like the Bodoni. To avoic
monotony of the straight lines of an ordina
sans serif the stems have slightly curved ou
typical of all Optima faces. This characteris
lends the various Optima designs their ele

message is necessarily e
difference, even though
designer plainly feels it
dreary old classic or otl
pography will infuse bri
dy? Surely it is illusory t
and technical capacity
in his rejection as bad r
not to be encouraged ir

A new slant

More radical is the addition of a true italic. Optima never had an italic form; its "italic" was essentially a sloped ver-sion of the roman (though carefully modeled so it looked much better than a mechanically slanted roman). In gen-eral, I'm not a big fan of sloped romans, because they're just not different enough from the roman to do their job of being a companion face; but of course Zapf's design for Optima italic was classic in its own right. Now he has given Optima a new italic, with different proportions and several very different letterforms. The swooping italic tail of the *f* and the one-storey *g*, along with the cursive *a*, *e*, and *l*, stand out dramatically. The other letters are nar-rower than their roman counterparts, and the whole face seems to have a steeper slant than the old Optima italic.

Optima nova italic, in the regular weight.

ABCDEFGHIJKLMNOPQRSTUVWXYZ
abcdefghijklmnopqrstuvwxyz
€ 1234567890 & 1234567890
Optima nova Italic

Linotype's brochure for Optima nova doesn't give us much to go on in judging the new italic; apart from the showings of the alphabet in each weight, there is only one

New letterforms in Optima nova include several cursive italic forms, and a revised numeral 1.

the lines carefully in varying short
and break lines within sentence
to reflect the dynami

Optima nova's startling italic (this is the bold italic) with its true italic forms.

ABCDEFGHIJKLMNOPQRSTUVWXYZ
abcdefghijklmnopqrstuvwxyz € 1234567890

Optima nova condensed, in the regular weight.

sample, a few lines in bold italic. There is no example of ordinary text with italic embedded in it.

The new italic is a handsome typeface, of course, but it's hard to think of it as Optima. Maybe I'm just too stuck in my ways, too used to the old Optima. But I'm skeptical of the new italic, as I am of the new semi-serif flares; they change the visual character of the face. The only way to find out, ultimately, whether they'll work or not is to put them to use and see how they look.

Additional refinements to Optima nova include small caps and old-style figures, which are very welcome indeed; and a condensed roman in five weights, which although unexpected will probably work well in practice. (There are no samples at all of the condensed face in use, in the brochure — just the alphabets.)

Finally, Zapf has designed a Titling version of Optima — a set of caps-only letters intended for use at large sizes, with lots of alternate forms and ligatures. Optima nova Titling's letters sprawl a little more than the regular ones do; in its optical relationship to the text face, it's reminiscent of Zapf's earlier display face Michelangelo, and that face's relationship to Palatino. The new Titling face is based on large letters that Zapf designed for a sculpture cast in aluminum, and like the aluminum letters, it has softly curved joins and interior angles. Instead of the added crispness of detail that you might expect of a face designed for display use, this one looks more sculptural.

On the money

The original inspiration for Optima came from Renaissance lettering carved into the floor of the church of Santa Croce in Florence, which the young Zapf was visiting in 1950. He had no paper with him, except Italian 1000-lira banknotes, so he sacrificed one of those (it was not a large sum) and made his initial sketches directly on the money. Not long ago he ran across this 1000-lira note again, and it became part of the exhibit at Zapfest

Optima nova Titling, with its ligatures and its rounded edges.

in San Francisco. The Optima nova brochure reproduces both sides of this historic bit of paper at full size, showing the pencil sketches that would eventually become Optima.

Optima has been an important part of the modern typographic palette for a long time. The purpose of Linotype's new version is to extend that long run well into the future. Despite my caveats about some aspects of Optima nova, I hope that this new version proves to be both useful and inspiring as a tool for typographers.

Some of Hermann Zapf's first sketches for Optima, made on an Italian banknote during his first visit to Italy in 1950.

HARMONIC SERIES
SIMONE DE BEAUVOIR
PREPOSITIONAL PHRASE
ELIZABETH MADOX ROBERTS

contemporary

Hoefler KO's specimen problems

Giving designers hands-on type samples is an uphill battle.

[*July 3, 2000*]

Cover of a type-specimen catalog from the Hoefler Type Foundry (now Hoefler & Frere-Jones).

THE OTHER DAY, a new typeface catalog from the Hoefler Type Foundry arrived in my mailbox. Entitled simply *Catalogue of Typefaces: Fourth Edition*, it reminded me that there are still a few type foundries that show their typefaces in generously designed, printed catalogs — and how important that is to designers looking for a good typeface to use.

This catalog is the size and format of a 48-page magazine. It has no frills, apart from a fine degree of typographic design. It's all black-and-white, except for a two-color cover (the back cover, also two-color, doubles as an order form), and it's printed on a fairly heavy white uncoated stock, stapled at the spine. There are only seven pages that aren't devoted to showings of the various type-faces for sale.

The Hoefler Type Foundry is the brainchild of Jonathan Hoefler, a prolific and extremely talented type designer in New York City. A decade ago, he was the wunderkind of the type world; while still in his teens, with a fresh-faced look that made him seem even younger than he was, he had become recognized as a masterful designer of typefaces in a surprising range of styles. Today, his business operates out of an address on lower Broadway, in SoHo, where he was recently joined by Tobias Frere-Jones, formerly of the Font Bureau.

When he was starting out, Hoefler had worked for Roger Black's studio, where he did a lot of work on designing or redesigning magazines; many of his type-faces were originally custom faces, commissioned as part of a redesign by magazines that would retain the exclu-sive right to use the faces for a year or two, after which

A showing of one of the typefaces in the Hoefler Type Foundry specimen book — in this case showing Leviathan.

Hoefler would be free to sell them to other customers. Not surprisingly, a lot of the typefaces in the Hoefler Type catalog are particularly useful for magazine headlines.

The poetry of headlines

In the catalog, every typeface, or at least every series or family, is given its own page to show off on. Hoefler has followed the old practice, seen in many type specimens from a hundred years ago, of choosing words and phrases that are colorful and attention-grabbing but that also happen to fit exactly into the space allotted for that typeface. For example, in showing Knockout No. 48 ("Featherweight"), he shows four lines all set in caps, in descending sizes (72pt, 60pt, 54pt, and 48pt), followed by two-line showings of smaller sizes, caps and lowercase. The first four lines read:

HARMONIC SERIES

SIMONE DE BEAUVOIR

PREPOSITIONAL PHRASE

ELIZABETH MADOX ROBERTS

Taken together, they don't make any sense, but they make an amusing if puzzling juxtaposition, and they do show precisely the right number of letters to fill each justified line. The whole book is full of this sort of stuff.

Bold, brawling Americans

Jonathan Hoefler has said that he's inspired by American wood type of the 19th century, and fascinated by the way the creators of this type would make series and families of big display letters that were obviously related but didn't stem from variations on some master design. The first type family he applied this idea to was Champion Gothic, a series of six heavy sans-serif typefaces based on 19th-century Grotesques and designed for headlines and other display uses in *Sports Illustrated*. Five of the six are condensed to various degrees, and they all look impressive at really huge sizes. If you look at any one letter and compare it across the six-face series (Hoefler chooses the **R** to show this), you can see that they're not just thickened or emaciated versions of the same letterform, but independent alphabets that work together.

The six styles of
HTF *Champion Gothic*

Fully a third of the catalog is devoted to showing off Hoefler's new variation on the same theme, a 32-member type family he calls Knockout. (Champion Gothic had a boxing theme; the weights were identifed as Bantamweight, Featherweight, Lightweight, Welterweight, Middleweight, and Heavyweight. In Knockout, he says, although each font has its boxing name, such as Junior Flyweight, it also sports a number: "Veteran Champion users will be happy to hear that they'll never again have to remember whether Welterweight comes before Middleweight.")

Knockout is "a new take on Champion Gothic," with an expanded range of widths and weights. It's also designed to work well in text, which the original was not. Like Champion Gothic, Knockout has that gawky, stark, artless look found in so many wood-type sans serifs. It cries out to be used in a boxing poster: "Frenchie Claude vs. Johnnie Bodoni! Saturday, Caslon Arena!"

European refinement
At the same time he produces these brawling display heavyweights, Jonathan Hoefler studies the finest details of elegant text faces and creates some remarkably thorough serif text families.

Hoefler Text was originally commissioned by Apple Computer to show off the capabilities of its TrueType GX technology. Hoefler tried a blend of characteristics from Garamond and Janson fonts, to create a sort of Ur-oldstyle typeface, then he gave it every variation under the sun: old-style figures, fractions, small caps, ligatures, "quaint" and "archaic" ligatures, math symbols, even refinements such as alternate versions of punctuation designed to work best with all caps or small caps. There are not one but two "engraved" versions of the caps, and a host of ornaments.

The samples show two sizes of text settings, along with display lines for every variation. This is also the typeface used for all the descriptive text throughout the catalog. Instead of the random phrases used to illustrate Knockout, Hoefler Text appears in blocks of text from Cicero's speech *In Catalinam* ("against Cataline") — a text used frequently in type specimens a couple of centuries ago.

Three of the twenty-seven fonts in the HTF *Hoefler Text family.*

HTF HOEFLER TEXT ROMAN
Quo usque tandem abutere, Catilina, patientia nostra? Quamdi

HTF HOEFLER TEXT ITALIC
Quamdiu etiam furor iste tuus nos eludet? Quem ad finem sese effrenata

HTF HOEFLER TEXT SWASH ITALIC
Iactabit Audacia? Nihilne Te Nocturum Præsidium Palatii, Nih

Another of the serif type families shown here is HTF Didot, which Hoefler calls "a historical revival in the French Neoclassical style." HTF Didot comprises 42 fonts, organized into seven series based on optical size; there's a 6 pt master, an 11 pt master, a 16 pt master, and so on up to 96 pt. The hairlines characteristic of Didot's typefaces are thick and robust in the tiniest sizes, thin and attenuated in the largest display size. Hoefler showed a more extensive sample of the whole family, with notes on how he designed it, in the first issue of his type magazine *Muse.*

Several optical sizes of
HTF *Didot*

The Hoefler Type Foundry's fourth catalog is a fine example of how a type foundry should show its wares. It's very much in the tradition of the best type specimen books from the days when foundries were big business and could afford thick, casebound books with a page or more for every typeface. The Hoefler catalog is actually dealing with no small type library — 141 separate fonts, by my count — but of course it's nothing like trying to show the entire Adobe library or the Agfa Monotype library, say.

Vendors of typefaces, whether the foundries themselves or resellers, face a dilemma: it costs a lot of money to publish a large printed catalog, and it's ever so much easier and cheaper to just show the fonts on the web — no paper, no ink, no printing, no shipping — but what every graphic designer wants is a real, physical, paper-and-ink catalog, one that you can hold in your hands and flip through. Unless you're designing exclusively for the screen, there's no substitute for seeing the typefaces used on paper, in as thorough and varied a way as possible. You really need fairly extensive showings, too, not just a single word or a phrase for each typeface. But producing even the most compact type catalog is a thankless task that can never pay for itself except in increased font sales.

So we should be glad when a type foundry takes the trouble to produce a well-made, well-thought-out catalog or specimen book like this one. There'll be well-thumbed copies on many an art director's desk in the coming year.

An American typeface

Nearly a decade after its release, John Downer's typeface Iowan Old Style finally possesses enough characters to be used in text.

[*February 9, 2001*]

BITSTREAM HAS FINALLY released the expert sets and related typographic refinements that make Iowan Old Style, a text family designed by John Downer in 1990 and originally released (without these) in 1991, usable in the way its designer intended.

Venice on the prairie

Iowan Old Style, despite the corn-fed sound of its name, has its roots deep in the Renaissance; Downer says that it's a Venetian old style, based on the types cut by Nicolas Jenson and Francesco Griffo in 15th-century Italy. It's a bit startling to see Iowan Old Style described as a Venetian, since the most prominent characteristic that distinguishes the Venetian faces from some of the slightly later Renaissance romans is the slanting crossbar of the lowercase **e**; the crossbar of the **e** in Iowan is straight. But the oblique stress, the low contrast between thick and thin strokes, the generous round letter shapes, and the calligraphic but blunt serifs do mark this face as related to Jenson's famous roman. As Bitstream describes it, "Iowan Old Style is a hardy contemporary text design modeled after earlier revivals of Jenson and Griffo typefaces but with a larger x-height, tighter letterfit, and reproportioned capitals." It is also modeled on "classical inscriptional lettering and sign painting seen in certain regions of eastern Iowa."

The typeface has a few features that remind me of Frederic Goudy's typefaces, such as the rounded-diamond shape of the dots over the **i** and **j**, and some of the curves in the italics. And of course Goudy's most well-known typeface is called Goudy Old Style (only one of many faces he designed that bear his name). But Iowan Old Style is smoother and less quirky than most of Goudy's highly individual designs.

Iowan Old Style has a very open look to its counters, with plenty of space inside the lowercase letters; yet its descenders and especially its ascenders are short, and it fits together fairly compactly. It's clearly a typeface made for reading in text.

What it takes to do the job

A text typeface needs more than just 26 letters and a handful of punctuation to be truly usable. An old-style text face, based on types that were first cut and used in books in the 15th to 18th centuries, should be accompanied by old-style figures, by a complete set of f-ligatures, and by true small caps. It ought to have a set of real fractions, too, or the numerators and denominators to create them. Without these, it looks as unconvincing as a callow Hollywood actor pretending to be a Shakespearean prince.

Iowan Old Style in use, with its new small caps & old-style figures.

IN THE SPRING OF 1935 – helped by Embeirikos, who had generously opened his large library to me – I became, awkwardly at first, the amazed observer of a strange world that leapt from my very being without my comprehension.

> – Odysseas Elytis, "T.T.T." (*Open Papers: Selected Essays,* trans. Olga Broumas & T Begley; Copper Canyon Press, 1995).

I don't know what misjudgment caused Bitstream to issue Iowan Old Style originally without any of these refinements (no doubt some mistake of marketing triage), but in 2000 they finally rectified their error by releasing a fairly extensive set of extra characters. Besides what I mentioned above, they included a number of accented letters beyond the usual Western set — enough to typeset Polish, Catalan, and Icelandic (though not, as far as I can see, Czech or Hungarian, except by using a

This Bitstream promotional graphic highlights Iowan Old Style's newly released small caps.

page-layout program to kern diacritical marks back over letters).

The type family also includes a handful of ornaments and two bolder weights (with their italics), Bold and Black. There are no italic small caps. (This is a traditional omission, but it invariably gets a designer in trouble when the design calls for small caps but the text calls for a word or title in italics.)

So nothing's perfect

There are some peculiarities to the way the supplementary fonts are arranged. The small caps font, for some unfathomable reason, has only small caps, and only in the lowercase positions — if you type a capital letter, all you get is a blank. I can't imagine why anyone would create a font like this, since so often we mix small caps and full caps in the same word or phrase. The italic alternates are given in a font that has nothing but them — not a full set of italics with the alternates replacing the appropriate letters. And there is no single font where the normal upper- and lowercase letters are combined with old-style figures.

To make use of these typographic refinements, you have to do a lot of replacing or reformatting of individual characters in a block of text, or a lot of careful search-and-replace operations if you're setting an entire book. Alternatively, you could pick and choose from the extended character set to create your own fonts with all the characters you need in one place.

Signs and books

John Downer is a sign painter and letterer as well as a skillful type designer, living and working in Iowa City. He recently released a set of fonts based on American painted signs of the 19th century, and he has been responsible for typefaces as varied as Triplex Italic (Emigre) and SamSans (Font Bureau). He would be better known, I think, as a designer of text types if Iowan Old Style had been issued in its complete form when it first came out.

Iowan Old Style cries out to be used in book work. It's a sturdy-looking, open, unfussy typeface with a narrower, contrasting italic, and it's readable down to very small sizes. Now that the necessary expert sets have been added to the available mix, perhaps we'll see it used more widely.

Warm modernism in profile

Martin Wenzel's typeface FF Profile shakes up our assumptions about sans-serif fonts.

[*August 3, 2001*]

ONE OF THOSE rules of thumb we love to repeat to ourselves, especially in the United States, is that sans-serif typefaces are inherently less readable in extended text than typefaces that have serifs. Sans serifs, the logic goes, are mechanical and lifeless; they've sacrificed the subtle warmth of an old-style serif typeface to the cold, cruel logic of the machine age. Yet this assumption has been challenged over recent decades by a significant number of type designers, most of them in Europe, who seem intent on creating a sort of warm modernism.

This detail from FontShop's FF Profile specimen book shows how a sans-serif typeface may be used in text.

> There is no direct inspiration for this one since it is not a revival. Classic and modern? Post-classical? Difficult to say. Certainly there are a few typefaces that have left an impression and subconsciously influenced the curves, straight lines and maybe even the kerning.
>
> Amongst them, Stempel Garamond with its generous proportions, outspoken shapes and occasional hard corner. It appears to me as very confident but not arrogant. Another contender has to be Berthold's Old Style version of the Bodoni with its strange crooked outlines. A beautiful, passionate design with –

The humanist tradition

FF Profile is one of a growing number of typefaces that are sans serif, monoline (or almost so), and characteristically clean and spare in appearance, but that have very little to do with either the clunky 19th-century tradition of serifless grotesques or the rational, modernist 20th-century tradition of geometrical sans serifs. This newly expanding category is the humanist sans serifs — typefaces whose letterforms are based on the humanist handwriting of the 15th century, or on the old-style type-

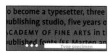

FontShop's FONT FOCUS *specimen book displays* FF *Profile in lowercase and small caps.*

faces that followed them (and that dominated printing until nearly the time of the French Revolution). Today's humanist sans serifs follow those Renaissance forms, but stripped of their ornamentation and most of their contrast, reduced to their essential forms and then reconstituted in a variety of weights. One characteristic of almost all humanist sans serifs is that they have true italics, not just slanted romans as so many other sans serifs do.

Martin Wenzel, the designer of FF Profile, is a 32-year-old German designer from Berlin who studied in the Netherlands and now works in Delft with Buro Petr van Blokland + Claudia Mens. Even if you didn't know that he'd been a student at the Royal Academy for Fine and Applied Arts, in the Hague, it would be obvious to anyone with an eye for the fine points of type that he'd been influenced by the humanist Dutch typographic tradition. Profile clearly grows out of some of the same ideas and concerns that gave us Petr van Blokland's Proforma and Luc(as) de Groot's Thesis. (It also has some details in common with Erik Spiekermann's Meta, which approaches the same problems from a somewhat different direction.)

The trick that a sans-serif typeface like this has to perform is to be varied enough for comfortable reading in long blocks of text, yet simple and unornamented enough to define its space on the page and suggest an uncluttered, modern, clearly delineated world.

I'm judging Profile entirely from printed samples; I've never put the fonts to use. And of course the new type-specimen booklet from FontShop (the fifth in their FontFont Focus series) is handsomely designed, in a way that would show any typeface off to its best advantage. The samples make me want to try out the face in various designs and layouts, much the way Thesis appealed to me the very first time I saw it. Profile has the same clarity and slim elegance that Thesis has, and a similarly open, spacious appearance. But Profile has a slightly warmer, less

Interesting FF Profile touches include an alternative "at" symbol that represents the symbol as a ligature of a and t.

stark look, because of detailing like the small, skewed swellings at the ends of some strokes. Without jumping around or being too lively, Profile possesses a slight informality that makes it feel friendly.

Fine details

Wenzel has given Profile humanist characteristics in the roman, such as the open aperture and small eye on the lowercase **a** and **e**, as well as a traditional two-story **g**. The italic, he points out, "is gently oblique and runs a little narrower and lighter than the respective roman." Both roman and italic are spaced generously, not crowded together like an advertising headline face. The ends of the some of the strokes are asymmetrical; in the **v**, for instance, the angles of the ends of the two arms are different.

Profile comes in five weights, each of which includes roman, italic, small caps, and no fewer than five different sets of numerals: old-style (the standard), lining, mono-spaced old-style (for tables and columns of figures, as in an annual report), and small lining figures in both the superscript and baseline positions (for making fractions, among other things). Wenzel has provided a number of simple but useful ornaments, such as arrows in various directions and dotted lines and boxes, as well as such unusual characters as a euro symbol with only one cross-bar (in addition to the standard one with two) and an alternate "at" sign that, as Wenzel puts it, "takes the 'at' literally, as a ligature of **a** and **t**." He even created appropriate versions of the various mathematical symbols that are part of every standard digital font, but that many type designers just let default to Symbol.

recipe

Take the forms of classical typefaces based on broad nibbed pen (for example, a Garamond).

The recipe

After describing some of the influences on the design of Profile (and making the usual disclaimer that it wasn't based directly on any particular face), Wenzel whimsically describes what he calls "the recipe":

"Take the forms of classical typefaces based on writing with a broad nibbed pen (for example, a Garamond). Then, carefully reduce the contrast within the character shapes (the thicks and the thins) to a minimum. To finish, reduce the serifs so that only a little detail will remind us that they were once there. Serve unscaled and with enough leading."

Not a bad recipe for the typographic cuisine of the 21st century. We have a lot of fine reading ahead of us.

The din of "undesigned" typefaces

Can the typefaces we see around us on highway signs be turned into usable fonts for general use? Sometimes.

[*December 15, 2001*]

FONTSHOP'S TYPE SPECIMEN BOOK for the FF DIN type family set me to thinking about so-called undesigned typefaces, especially those derived from the letters used on highway signs.

The conceit is that these typefaces are simpler, more straightforward, and somehow more honest than faces with subtler curves and fine serifs and a visible pedigree from the history of type design. They look functional. And hey, they must be functional, right? They're used on highway signs!

FF DIN is based on the German industry standard ("Deutsche Industrie Norm") for signage on the Autobahn.

Industry type

"DIN" stands for "Deutsche Industrie Norm," which means exactly what it looks like it means: German industry standard. The standards apply to many areas beyond type, but DIN has taken on a symbolic importance in the realm of German public lettering. FF DIN is based on DIN-Mittelschrift, a ubiquitous signage face that FontShop calls "the German 'Autobahn' typeface." The original DIN-Mittelschrift is a clunky design, "a spotty typeface with quirky letterforms," devoid of any character except its artlessness. It is, however, legible.

Albert-Jan Pool, a Dutch designer working in Hamburg, took on the challenge of reworking DIN-Mittelschrift to give it a little bit of typographic elegance, and expanding it into a type family of several weights, so that

Font Bureau's Interstate, based on U.S. freeway signs, has proven extremely popular.

it might become a usable part of the typographer's palette for all kinds of of graphic design, in text as well as display. He even created an italic ("a combination of rationality and emotion"), a condensed (with the aid of other designers, scrupulously credited in the specimen book), old-style figures, and a few alternate characters, for those "looking for slightly less severity in a face." The result is a "rational"-appearing typeface that is more readable than the original DIN types but still evokes all the associations with German industrial engineering. (Interestingly, the specimen book mentions specifically that FF DIN has become popular with designers "working for labels that promote contemporary music.")

The street has its uses

FF DIN is not the only typeface derived from road signs. Font Bureau's Interstate family, based on the typeface used on those green freeway signs that punctuate the U.S. interstate highway system, has been extremely popular. Tobias Frere-Jones adapted it in 1993–94; since then, he and Cyrus Highsmith have expanded it into what Font Bureau calls "a plethora of enticing styles." Like FF DIN, it gives the impression of being raw, but it's a lot more elegant than its source.

James Montalbano's ClearviewOne is an attempt at a real signage face — a better alternative to the clunky Interstates and DINs. So far I've seen it used quite successfully in text, but I haven't followed its allure down an actual highway.

Mark van Bronkhorst developed the Conduit family for ITC in 1997. ITC Conduit goes after the same sort of artlessness as Interstate or DIN; van Bronkhorst saw it as the lettering that an untrained person might draw on the side of a boiler. (Its letterforms even look a little like steam pipes.)

Faux naïf

All of the faces I've named, except perhaps some of their roadside originals, are well designed and executed. But a typeface derived from signage isn't always suitable for text. A few years ago, the designer of science-fiction writer William Gibson's novel *Virtual Light* used a highway-signage typeface as the text face for the book. Yes, it was legible. But the typeface didn't distinguish very well between the period and the comma—and Gibson's style makes very precise use of both.

Highway-signage type used for the text of a novel? Go back! You are going wrong way!

> They used this big specialty car wash off Colby: twenty coats of hand-rubbed Wet Honey Sienna and you didn't let it get too shabby.
>
> That one November evening the Republic of Desire put an end to his career in armed response. Berry Rydell had arrived there a little early.
>
> He liked the way it smelled inside. They had this pink stuff they put through the power-washers to get the road film off, and the smell reminded him of a summer job he'd had in Knoxville, his last year in school. They'd been putting condos into the shell of this big

What is the appeal of these typefaces? They give the illusion of not really being designed at all, so using them in print reinforces the idea of naïve authenticity and unstudied design.

This is all nonsense, of course; it's just a look, a style. But it's a style as useful as any other, and sometimes it's appealing and perfectly appropriate. When you need a typeface that evokes this kind of feeling, one of these fonts might do the trick.

From the invitation for the exhibition "Italic 1.0," using Fabrizio Schiavi's typeface CP Company.

A new slant on "italic"

The impressive catalog of "Italic 1.0," an exhibition in Rome that coincided with the 2002 ATypI conference, opens a window on contemporary type design in Italy.
[*December 2, 2002*]

WHILE ITALY IS the home of the roman letter (and its sidekick the italic), and Italian industrial and graphic design were legendary for much of the 20th century, modern Italy has not been at the forefront of the art of type design. But this is clearly changing. The bilingual book *Italic 1.0: il disegno di caratteri contemporaneo in italia/ contemporary type design in Italy* (Milano: AIAP Edizioni, 2002), which serves as the catalog of an exhibition that was shown in Rome in September 2002, shows off the variety and quality of the type design being created today in Italy. The exhibition coincided with the 2002 ATypI conference, and attendees had the opportunity (if they could tear themselves away from the conference's multiple tracks of programming on Italian and international typography) to see both "Italic 1.0" and a companion exhibition, "5 Masters of Italian Graphics," at the National Library in Rome.

I never managed to get to the exhibitions, much to my regret, but the catalog of "Italic 1.0" is an impressive introduction. It's a well-made 120-page book, in A4 format on a comfortably toothy off-white paper stock that takes color printing very well yet feels like a book, not a glossy magazine. The design accommodates a wide variety of showings, both horizontal and vertical, of typefaces and their uses, organized into short chapters (of one to three spreads) on each of 25 designers.

Two types
The two typefaces used for the text are both the work of type designers featured in the book, but they are radically

*Giovanni de Faccio's
typeface Rialto, in use in the
bilingual catalog for
"Italic 1.0."*

different from each other. The main text and the bio-graphical notes on the designers use Giovanni de Faccio's Rialto, an elegant, lively calligraphic face rooted in Italian Renaissance type, which features subtly different versions that are suitable for text at various sizes. (I had admired Rialto when I first saw it, but I thought it might be too lively to work as a versatile text face. It isn't; its use in this book proves that it does work very well in text, and I could easily imagine putting it to good use in the design of books.)

In contrast, the descriptions of each typeface are presented in CP Company, an industrial sans serif designed by Fabrizio Schiavi as a corporate typeface for a clothing company; the CP Company family is intended to be legible onscreen as well as on the printed page, and its simplified, slightly squarish forms contrast surprisingly well with the elegant Rialto. (CP Company is also used as a headline face for the names of the designers on each spread.) All of the text is bilingual, first in Italian and then in English, but the distinction is made purely by position of the text blocks; there is no typographic distinction between the languages. (In the two introductory essays, there is one more distinguishing element: the English runs across the bottom half of the page, in black, while the Italian runs across the top, in a dark reddish-brown ink that's used effectively throughout the book.)

A typographic explosion

I keep coming back to the word "variety." Any survey of type designs will show a wide variation in approach, style, and execution, but *Italic 1.0* covers a very wide range indeed. We find elegant, carefully crafted serif text faces like Rialto or Jane Patterson & John Downer's Simona (yes, a few of the type designers are non-Italians who, like Patterson, work in Italy; some of the others are Italians who work outside Italy); purely calligraphic typefaces like Anna Ronchi's Etruria and Mulino Bianco; signage

Scipio, by Giovanni Lussu, cast in bronze.

type based on ancient Roman incised lettering (Giovanni Lussu's Scipio, which has been cast in bronze and used in plaques along the pedestrian route between the Pantheon and the Trevi Fountain); and cheerful eccentricities like the distressed Apocalisse ("Apocalypse") from the Milan design studio Jekyll & Hyde, or Enrico Baldetti's Jolly-music with its curly dots, which will clearly look right at home on a music flyer or CD cover.

A few of the designers, such as Fabrizio Schiavi, Alessio Leonardi, Antonio Pace, and Albert Pinggera, are already familiar to international audiences because their type designs have been published by internationally known font distributors like Linotype, FontShop, or T-26.

Up front

Two essays lead off the book: "Dopo Novarese / After Novarese," by Mario Piazza and Silvia Sfigliotti, and "Caratteri moderni / Contemporary type" by Carlo Branzaglia.

Aldo Novarese's hands (in photograph) and samples of some of his typefaces.

The first essay takes its title from the hugely influential Aldo Novarese, head of the Artistic Studio at the Nebiolo type foundry for half a century, but the writers look both forward and back from Novarese (who died in 1995), showing both the effect he had and the limitations that he labored under. Piazza and Sfigliotti make the case that Italian typography suffered from a long split between graphic design and type, where graphic designers neither learned much about type nor thought it very important, and where the expertise of type designers like Novarese wasn't valued in the successful halls of indus-

A page of "Alberobanana," an imagined alternate version of how our alphabet might have developed.

trial design. This has only changed, they say, in the last decade, with the flowering of independent digital type-design studios and the creation of a market for new type designs for corporations and cultural institutions.

The second essay takes off from the influence that Neville Brody's design of *The Face* in the UK in the 1980s had on art directors everywhere, including Italy, bringing home the realization that type was an integral part of graphic design. But Branzaglia's essay veers too far into the academic in style, at the same time that it jumps around in subject, trying to touch on as many of the designers included in the exhibition as possible.

A third introductory piece isn't an essay so much as a visual experiment: "Alberobanana." Alessio Leonardi developed the Alberobanana project, he says, for a conference on typography and religion. As a kind of thought experiment, he imagined that the Phoenicians had picked different symbols for each of their letters — so that, for instance, the letter that became our **A** started out not as a cow but as a tree — and he then let these alternative symbols evolve along the same lines as our real letters did. So he came up with variations like Alberobanana Onciale (in the medieval Uncial style), Alberobanana Bodoni (you guessed it), and even Alberobanana Franklin Gothic. This concept, which is given a single spread in the book, is amusing and perhaps thought provoking, although in essence it's the same process followed by any type designer adapting a type style from the Latin script to, say, Greek or Cyrillic.

Everyone who attended the ATypI conference in Rome came away with a copy of *Italic 1.0* (whether they got to the exhibition at the National Library or not), but for the rest, I suggest either buying the book through Nijhof & Lee in Amsterdam, who were selling it there as the conference's official book dealer, or getting in touch with the publisher directly. It is well worth adding to your working bookshelf.

Industrial cool

In its catalogs and type specimens, House Industries has made its retro style up-to-the-minute.

[*February 15, 2002*]

THE LATEST product catalog from House Industries, the Delaware-based digital type foundry with its heart in the early 1960s, makes their expansion of the House Gothic family seem stylish, poised, and inevitable. These guys (as far as I know, they're all men) are masters of presentation.

House Industries' House Gothic 23.

HOUSEGOThIC23

Cool, calm, resurrected
The catalog (*House Industries Product Catalog No. 28*) is largely a promotional piece and type specimen for House Gothic 23, the once-nuclear type family, originally released in 1996, that has now grown into a 23-member extended family so big that the kids are spilling out of the house. A square, 20-page brochure, printed in coordinated shades of tan and brown, this catalog has only four pages that aren't directly devoted to House Gothic 23 (and one of those is a page extolling "House Textiles," an upcoming line of fabrics, which kicks off with a throw pillow printed in a pattern based on House Gothic's egg-cup-like letter **x**).

A swatch from House Textiles.

House Industries' graphic style is derived almost entirely from the "modern" graphic styles of America in the late '50s and early '60s: sleek, streamlined, forward-looking, the sort of look celebrated in the "Century 21" graphics of the 1962 World's Fair in Seattle. (They also have fun with other retro '60s styles, in type families like the Las Vegas Font Collection, the Rat Fink Fonts, the Tiki Type Collection, and Typography of Coop. Their love affair with the early '60s reached its apotheosis in the Chalet Font Family, ostensibly based on the designs of the mythical clothing designer René Albert Chalet.) The phrases they use to describe various styles of House Gothic are telling: "stylish yet functional," "a sense of sophistication and elegance," "at once forceful and suave," "a debonair sense of style." Hipsters, take note.

This modernistic style was still in use in the late '60s, though by then it had been absorbed into the mainstream and looked a little old-hat. I recently dug out a reduced-size Rand McNally Road Atlas from 1969, the kind that was given away as a freebie by companies who'd put their logo on it, in which the typographic style is pure House Gothic — or rather, what House Gothic acknowledges and exaggerates.

A rising x-height floats all fonts

The House designers have taken their fashion statement, House Gothic, and turned it into what they hope is a complete typographic solution — one of those type families that can fulfill all your needs in a complex project. Within the limits of the squarish, stripped-down, bent-wire look that the typeface embodies, they may well have achieved it. I don't have the fonts themselves — just the promotional brochure — but they look versatile. In any case, they've certainly been presented well, in a way that makes you want to buy them and use them. That's what promotional materials are for, after all. It's a pleasure to see them done well.

The four faces of House Gothic.

House Gothic is not only a sans-serif typeface design with squarish curves, in the style of Aldo Novarese's Microgramma and Eurostile, but also a variation on the concept of a unicameral typeface: a typeface where capital and lowercase letter styles mix at the same x-height, with hardly any extenders. But House Gothic takes this concept a step farther. There are actually four different versions of each of the House Gothic styles; style 1 has a large x-height but normal forms to the lowercase letters, while the x-height increases progressively in styles 2 and 3, until with style 4 the x-height equals the cap height in all but a few of the letters. The effects are subtly different; this is a mode of variation that I haven't seen before.

To round out the family, the House designers added three text versions (light, italic, and bold), where the more extreme characteristics of the display styles have been toned down to be readable at text sizes. Although the loopy **x** and **w** might have benefited from more traditional alternate versions (which exist, oddly, for some of the display fonts), the body copy in this brochure is definitely readable. (It's all set in 8pt House Gothic 23 Text Light, on 14pt leading. Because of the very large x-height, the type looks much bigger than its nominal point size.)

Sample of House Gothic Text Light

Today's designer is often faced with the enormous task of creating complex layout solutions without jeopardizing stylistic values. Common typographic formulae eschew the objectives that they seek to fulfill as the need for utility often overshadows the

The way the future was

Of course, the style that House Gothic is based on was futuristic in 1962; today it's nostalgic. The only way we've come to that envisioned world of the future is by our fetish for the retro. But the urge to create clean, uncluttered designs is a constant one; it can produce graphic

House Gothic 23 freshens old font contours.

effects that look fresh while simultaneously alluding to older attempts at the same thing. Some of the details of the letter shapes in House Gothic, like the sharp corners and the straight stroke in the central curve of the **s**, also bring to mind Neville Brody's display typefaces for The Face in the 1980s.

It would be interesting to see House Gothic 23 used in ways that run counter to its inspiration. What would happen if you combined the light weights with a few carefully chosen words or letters in a highly embellished Spencerian script? Or blackletter text with House Gothic headlines? (Maybe I'm getting carried away.) The retro-clean look is one way to use typefaces like these — one that House Industries has embodied with panache in this catalog — but sometimes it's interesting to try mixing things up.

Ample scope for typography

A big type family thrives on a life of a thousand cuts.
[*July 10, 2003*]

Font Bureau, which is known for extensive type families with a lot of visual character that work especially well in publication design, has released a 35-member family called Amplitude, designed by Christian Schwartz. I can only guess that it got named "Amplitude" because of its wide range of styles: seven weights in five widths, from Ultra Wide to Light Extra Compressed (and, conversely, from Light Wide to Ultra Extra Compressed). It might also reflect the way most of the variations can be used at many sizes from tiny text to huge display; Amplitude is one of those robust sans-serif typefaces whose details make it readable at small sizes while giving it a recognizable character at large sizes. In this case, the distinctive features of the face come from design details that are intended to keep it legible at very small sizes indeed.

Crystalline agate
Amplitude features "light traps": knife-like cuts in the angles of some letters that keep the ink from filling in the narrow spaces and making the type look blobby when printed at small sizes on rough paper. At tiny sizes, readers don't notice the light traps; all they see is that the type can be read easily. If you blow the same letters up to large size, however, all the details like light traps become very obvious. (When I was a typesetter in a phototype shop in the late '70s, we had a version of itc American Typewriter produced by Compugraphic that was meant for use at text sizes; we also had a separate machine, a "headliner," for setting display sizes, with a separate filmstrip of display American Typewriter. If, instead of using the headliner, you used the lenses of the text machine to blow up the text version of this monoline, round-ended

Font Bureau's type specimens of Amplitude, showing the letters' characteristics, including exaggerated light traps.

typeface to display size, it looked like a string of sausages, or a balloon sculpture.)

Schwartz observed the way these "entirely functional compensations" worked in the typefaces known as "agates," specialized faces created for the very tiniest type in newspapers — for things like stock listings, which have to be clear and unambiguous but also have to take up as little space as possible — and he turned these peculiarities into features that give the typeface a distinctive look at larger sizes. Then he expanded this specialized idea into a very large type family.

There's clearly a demand for typefaces like this; and the malleable nature of digital fonts makes it easy to take typefaces that were designed for use at one particular size and use them at any size at all. A number of publication designers have used the old Bell Gothic, designed by C. H. Griffith in 1938 to be a functional hot-metal type for setting the listings in U. S. telephone directories, as a contemporary headline face. At large sizes, those little details become exaggerated and draw attention to themselves and their quirkiness — which is exactly the effect the designers who use the faces are after.

Font Bureau has capitalized on this demand once before, when Tobias Frere-Jones designed an updated type family, called Griffith Gothic, based on C. H. Griffith's original. Amplitude fits right into the same niche. But Griffith Gothic is a more playful face than Amplitude, with rounder forms; Amplitude also partakes of the current taste for slightly squarish forms in its rounder characters.

Invaded by space
Some of the sharp details of Amplitude look arbitrary at large sizes: the light traps in the capital **Z**, for example, especially in the Bold, Black, and Ultra versions. (All of these details are more noticeable in the heavier weights.) But others simply look chiseled and give the letters an

interesting texture when you see them large. While the knife-thin light traps at the interior angles of **A** and **M** make those letters look oddly wounded, the white wedges intruding into the black shapes of letters like **g**, **n**, and **r** give them character.

I don't think the designer had this in mind, but when I was looking at the showings of Amplitude on the Font Bureau website, I noticed how sharp it looked onscreen. This is not the same as a typeface designed specifically as a screen font, for use in text sizes at low resolution, but I suspect that Amplitude would work well at display sizes and large-text sizes in onscreen design.

Amplitude is designed to fit a lot of words onto a line; most of its widths are at the Condensed end of the spectrum, and even the Normal width is narrow. Only the Wide version has a generous text width; in that, it reminds me of Ole Schäfer's FF Fago, another large family of squarish sans serifs where the "wide" is what I'd call a normal width. While I wouldn't want to see Amplitude's narrowest widths used at small sizes, this abundance of slim options could make it very useful as a headline face.

Interrogatory, my dear Watson

Although Amplitude doesn't have an unusually extensive character set, it does include the double-**f** ligatures (**ff**, **ffi**, **ffl**) along with the common **fi** and **fl**; and it has three oddities: an *interrobang* (a combination of exclamation point and question mark in the same punctuation mark, which was introduced as a concept — one that didn't catch on — in the 1950s) and two original variations which might be called an *interrocomma* and a *commabang*. As you can guess, these last two incorporate a comma in place of the dot at the bottom of the question mark and the exclamation point. What real use they might have is hard to imagine, but they're in the fonts.

personalities

The world on the page

How one French type designer affects the daily life of the readers of France.

[*January 5, 2001*]

Jean-François Porchez

JEAN-FRANÇOIS PORCHEZ has been redefining the day-to-day typography of France for several years from his bedroom.

The 36-year-old type designer and typographer has had a remarkably wide influence on the look of printed matter in France. Rather than establishing a flashy, distinctive style in advertising, and making his mark that way, Porchez has instead had the opportunity to rework the appearance of some of his country's most widely-read newspapers — and part of the signage of one of the world's best-known subway systems, the Paris Métro.

Specimen of the Le Monde type family, in the form of a mocked-up newspaper front page.

Le Monde

The most respected daily newspaper in Paris is *Le Monde*, which is often referred to by Americans as "the *New York Times* of France." *Le Monde* matches the *Times* in portentousness and giving the impression of speaking with ineffable authority, but it does so with a good deal more candor and enthusiastic analysis.

Typographically, *Le Monde* also resembles the *Times* in the jumbled look of its front page, although it goes the

*A comparison of the letter-
forms of Le Monde Journal
and Times Roman.*

Times one better by mixing serif and sans-serif text typefaces as well as using a variety of headline styles. When
Jean-François Porchez was called upon to design a new
typeface for the esteemed newspaper, he created a super-
family comprising both serif and sans-serif type families
that were designed to work together — and to work on
the crowded, quickly printed pages of a daily newspaper.
(Naturally, the way his typefaces are actually used every
day is a lot more chaotic than the carefully thought-out
sample he designed to show off how the typefaces could
be made to work together.)

Le Monde Journal, the serif typeface that debuted
in *Le Monde* in 1995, bears an obvious and intentional
resemblance to Times New Roman (which was the serif
text face of the newspaper before the introduction of
Porchez's typefaces). Like Times, Le Monde is narrow
without looking so. But it has a larger x-height and a
somewhat larger "eye," to give more space inside the letters. There's a little more sparkle and liveliness to the cut
of the letters, but not enough to be distracting. The italic
is more calligraphic than the Times italic, and not so
curly — all of which helps its legibility, both within a passage of roman text and when used by itself.

Le Monde Sans — which is frequently used on its own
in the daily newspaper — is also calligraphic, but not obviously so. It has an oblique stress, like the serif face, and
subtle variation in the weight of the strokes. And it has a
true italic (unlike the slanted roman of, say, Helvetica).

Porchez has extended the family with several other
subfamilies: Le Monde Livre, a bookface based on Le
Monde Journal but modified to work at larger text sizes,
and Le Monde Courrier, an informal slab-serif typeface
meant for correspondence (in the tradition of faces such
as ITC Stone Informal). More recently, Porchez has
extended Le Monde Livre still further with Le Monde
Livre Classic, which adds a large number of historical

1 Le Monde Livre
2 Le Monde Livre Classic

*Le Monde Livre (left)
and swash characters of
Le Monde Livre Classic
(right).*

letterforms, ligatures, ornaments, swashes, and variations to the basic book family.

Other newspapers
When I visited Porchez, at his small apartment in
Malakoff, an industrial suburb on the southern outskirts
of Paris, he was working on the re-design of a line of
regional newspapers in the middle of the country. He
showed me his work in progress, as well as several earlier
typographic makeovers he had performed on other
French periodicals.

Newspapers in the provinces are not usually at the
cutting edge of journalistic design, but they are workhorses that are read by thousands and thousands of
people every day. How those papers look, and how easy
they are to read, is essential to their success. It's hard to
think of any undertaking more "unsung" than the one
Porchez took on, yet by doing it he had an immediate,
direct, hands-on effect on the daily experience of his
countrymen.

Homework
Like many independent type designers, Jean-François
Porchez works from home. The image of the mighty
Porchez Typofonderie may be seamlessly professional —
and it does accurately reflect the quality of the work —
but the actual labor was being done at a Mac on a desk
in the half of the bedroom that was designated his work
space. Since he was sharing his home with his wife and
two small children, the boundaries of the workspace
were purely theoretical — though strictly maintained.
(The boundary-keeping went both ways. His posters
and type samples and books could not slop over into the
living space.)

Parisine in use in the Paris Métro (top), and part of a specimen of the enlarged Parisine type family (above).

Parisine

The other area where Porchez has had a typographic effect on daily life is in his typeface for the Paris Métro, called Parisine. Parisine is used both on signage and on maps and other printed materials.

There is more than one typeface in use in the Métro, and Porchez is following in the footsteps of one of the 20th century's great typographic practitioners: Adrian Frutiger designed the earlier signage typeface, which is still in common use. I confess that when I've ridden the Paris Métro I've been hard put to figure out the logic behind the use of the two typefaces (there are also older remnants of earlier lettering, as there are in almost any subway system that's been around for a while), but the general direction-finding system is noticeably more coherent in Paris than it is in, say, New York. Of course, the typeface has only so much influence on this; everything depends on how the typeface is actually used. (And on how logical the actual arrangement of the lines, the stations, and the trains really is. No signage or way-finding system can make up for a physically confusing transit system.)*

La voix de la lettre

Porchez is an activist in the field of typography. He organizes and supports design events in Paris, he teaches widely, and he organized the program of the 1998 ATypI conference in Lyons. He is matter-of-fact and unpretentious, but he has strong opinions. He takes a resolutely international stance on typography, yet he has also been instrumental in bringing together and publicizing the typography and typographers of France, in ventures such as the encyclopedic small book prepared for the Lyons conference, *Lettres françaises*.

He is also one hell of a type designer.

*For more about subway signage, see *Dot-font: talking about design* (Mark Batty Publisher, 2006).

Robert Norton

Innovative, meticulous, and irreverent, Robert Norton was responsible for the surprising quality of the typefaces issued by Microsoft.

[*April 13, 2001*]

Robert Norton, innovator and type designer.

FOR A FEW SHORT YEARS in the early 1990s, Robert Norton had a decisive influence on something we all use and we all take for granted: the typefaces that accompanied Microsoft's Windows operating system and a whole slew of Microsoft software products.

Norton, who died in England on March 8, 2001, brought a lifetime of typographic knowledge to the task of overseeing Microsoft's development of TrueType fonts — a small part of Microsoft's business, but one with a very wide influence, precisely because of the reach of Microsoft products.

He was "the cornerstone of Microsoft's type group," as Nicolas Barker put it in his obituary in the *Independent*: "responsible for the selection and creation of all the typefaces for Windows, Word, Office, Encarta, and all other Microsoft programs."

Substance with style

Norton's stint at Microsoft could be considered just a coda to a long life in the typographic world. Because of his long experience — not just a knowledge of type but a personal history of putting new typesetting technologies to profitable use — he brought to the Microsoft type group a depth of knowledge and taste that it couldn't easily create for itself. Despite his skepticism about the gung-ho world of software developers, "his integrity" (to quote Barker again) "stayed unchanged as his intellect wrestled with the task of preserving the individuality of letter-designs within the Microsoft straitjacket."

Robert Norton's irreverent type glossary, for Microsoft.

Norton's wit, with which he obliquely but relentlessly tried to deflate pretension, including his own, showed up in the most unlikely places — even in the User's Guides to Microsoft's packages of TrueType fonts. Introducing a brief description of Eurostile, one of the typefaces adapted to TrueType for Microsoft's Font Pack 2, he began, "Almost every graphic design student has at one time or another tried a hand at a geometrical type. Few have made anything remotely memorable." Or, describing the very boldest, heaviest face in the Gill Sans family, Gill Sans Ultra Bold: "There's a lot of fun in this face, which is also known as Gill Kayo. In a sinking boat, you wouldn't want to read directions in Gill Sans Ultra Bold telling you how to put on your life jacket. But if a sign said stop [this one word is printed, in the guide, in the typeface itself], you would probably stop, even if you normally are not very obedient."

In its combining of irreverence and historical erudition, Norton's style is unmistakable. On Baskerville Old Face: "This face is based on one developed by the renowned 18th-century typographer John Baskerville. But tell-tale differences, including the characteristic squarish curves in the capital **C** and **G**, identify it as the version first issued by the Fry type foundry, established by the Fry family after they succeeded in the chocolate business. The face first appeared in 1766 under the name of Isaac Moore, the foundry manager."

Best remembered

I knew Robert Norton only briefly, during his stint in the suburban fringe of Seattle. He was a huge man, six foot six and "broad to match," with a large head and a shambling gait. He took delight in applying his typographic skills and knowledge to the problems of choosing and judging the fonts that Microsoft would issue, but in that environment of young software whizkids he seemed a little like a fish out of water. He brought me in at one

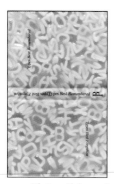

The two-sided cover of Robert Norton's back-to-back *Types Best Remembered/Types Best Forgotten*

point for a short stint evaluating the outlines for a bunch of typefaces being considered, but while I was there, I was, for the most part, actually dealing with other, more technical people. I would occasionally go out to lunch with Robert, where we might talk about the job at hand or about anything else under the sun. I'm only sorry I didn't see more of him after that particular project was through. I did manage to get him, a few times, to attend an informal group of people in Seattle who liked to get together and talk about type. He was always excellent company.

He was oddly self-deprecating for someone so accomplished. After his wonderfully eccentric little book *Types Best Remembered / Types Best Forgotten* came out, he told me that he had sent me an invitation to be one of the contributors (each of whom named one typeface they thought should be commemorated, and one they'd like to see discarded forever), "but you probably filed it in the round file." He affected not to believe that I might have never received his invitation in the first place. (I would have been very happy to contribute. I can easily imagine — all too easily — letting such an letter sit on my desk too long while I thought about the best way to approach the problem, but I would never have simply forgotten it.)

That book was a fine example of his ingenuity, too. He had taken to publishing small books like that himself, at odd intervals, and making their production cheaper by dealing with printers that he knew were doing large jobs; he would find out what size page could be printed on the extra paper that would otherwise be trimmed and thrown away, and adjust the format of his book accordingly. This meant less than ideal control over what kind of paper he could use, but it did make it possible for the books to come out, without the intervention of a large publisher.

The small books of the facetiously but aptly named Parsimony Press.

A flair for business

Robert Norton spent much of his life in the business of type, although he managed to punctuate it with long-distance sailing trips and with such early adventures as living by his wits in New York City and establishing a bookshop and a factory in Jamaica. Sensing the possibilities of the new technology of phototypesetting, he established, with a partner, what Nicolas Barker calls "an innovative firm that combined phototypesetting with an instant print service," and he became adept at making his own film-strips for the new typesetting systems. In 1982 he designed the type family Else, a modern-style typeface in the Century Old Style tradition. He developed techniques for adapting typefaces for use in early desktop laser printers — not only for the Latin alphabet but for Hebrew, Arabic, Tibetan, and Japanese.

His last venture, after he left Microsoft in 1997, put his skills in publishing to work again. He went home to England and established Parsimony Press (*www.parsimony.co.uk*) with Andrew Pennock, to publish small, inexpensive, elegantly designed gift books for the intelligent reader. "We will try to make no books whose contents are not proper furniture for an enquiring and mischievous mind," claims the Parsimony website — another clear example of Norton's inimitable flair. The new business was simultaneously quixotic and hard-headed: giving away samples to booksellers, the way a new chocolatier might send free samples to prospective vendors of his product, with the idea that if enough demand was created, the books could be produced in large numbers at very little cost, and sold for the price of a greeting card.

True to type, at the very end of his life Robert Norton established another innovative business, one that may well long outlive him.

The readable designer

Thirty years of Gerard Unger's highly legible text and display typefaces can now be seen together on his website.

[*February 7, 2003*]

Gerard Unger (top), and one of his type designs used for road signage in the Netherlands (above).

GERARD UNGER'S typeface designs have added both style and legibility to any number of publications. Until now, however, his influence has been less obvious than it might be, because his work is scattered in so many places. The debut of his own new website (*www.gerardunger.com*) concentrates examples of all of his work in one place, making it easier to see both the forest and the trees. It's also a well-designed site with a lot of useful information.

Type for everyday use
Unger's best-known typefaces are probably Swift (1985), Amerigo (1986), and Flora (1984). His newspaper face Gulliver (1993) is familiar to millions of readers, as it's the typeface used in both *USA Today* and several European newspapers; but newspaper readers seldom know the name of the typeface they're reading, and Gulliver is not generally available except to large publishing houses. If you live in the Netherlands, you probably see Unger's letters almost every day; he has designed typefaces for the signage systems of both the Dutch highways and the Amsterdam metro.

Most of Unger's type designs, however, are text faces, even if many of them will also work at display sizes. They tend to combine well with each other; he has designed sans-serif type families that complement his serif families (Oranda with Amerigo, for instance, or Praxis with Demos), but even the less obviously related faces of his seem to work togther. He has updated some of his earlier type designs, which were created for cruder digital typesetting systems or for use on lower-quality paper: Demos

(1976) was redigitized and revised in 2001 for the German government, and Swift (1985) has been upgraded to a new version, Swift 2.0.

Unger has always worked with the constraints of technology in mind, and he is quite articulate about how and why he created particular features of his typefaces. One of the first typefaces he designed was called M.O.L. "This type for signage on the Amsterdam metro," says Unger, "was designed in collaboration with a workgroup led by Pieter Brattinga. As a fair proportion of the signs are illuminated from within, using fluorescent tubes, the principles of optics were taken as the basis for the design. Whatever form an opening has — triangular, square or polygonal — the light shining through it onto a surface always tends to form a circle. M.O.L. is rounded throughout as a device to make illuminated lettering more even and legible. This was the first type design in which I started experimenting with the counters of letters (the spaces within the letters) by making them larger as a way of improving legibility."

Unger's playfulness is evident in this footnote to the description of M.O.L.: "Mol is the Dutch word for a mole. The workgroup had come up with the idea of a mole as a mascot for the new underground railway. Outside every station in the city there would be a giant molehill with a mole pointing the way to the entrance with his nose. The idea was torpedoed by the city authorities, but we let it live on in the name of the typeface."

The thick and thin of it
Unger's typefaces are distinctive. Even when he designs very different kinds of letters, the forms tend to bear a family resemblance to each other. Most of his typefaces are upright and sturdy; even the most refined could be described as typographic workhorses. This is squarely in the tradition of Dutch type design, which gave us many of the useful text typefaces of the 17th century — and many of the useful text faces of the late 20th. As he notes in talking about M.O.L., Unger pays careful attention to the spaces within each letter and to the spaces between letters. The interplay of stroke and background is integral to type design — quite consciously so in the work of Gerard Unger.

But Unger's fascination with that interplay also shows up in the form of the strokes he draws to make each letter. His strokes tend to come to points, not only at the ends of serifs but where one stroke meets another within a letter. This gives a sparkle and liveliness to the letters when they're set large, and makes it especially easy to distinguish different forms when they're set small in text. Sometimes the joins between strokes get so thin that they almost seem to disappear. He has experimented with this phenomenon to see how much can be taken away and still be legible; the font that he created for FontShop's *Fuse* 2, called Decoder (1992), uses bits and pieces of his typeface Amerigo to make a pattern of shapes that pushes the limits of what can comfortably be read.

Unger deconstructed one of his own type designs to see how much of legibility is just a matter of suggestion.

All the type that's fit for news

Several of Unger's typefaces have been designed as text faces for newspapers. As a result (or perhaps as a cause), he has given a great deal of thought to what makes a typeface readable in that unforgiving format. In discussing his recent design Coranto (2000), he notes: "Over the past twenty-five years newspaper production has seen spectacular improvements in paper and print quality, the introduction of colour printing, and vastly better register. These changes have gone almost unnoticed, having been largely overshadowed by the arrival of the Internet. For text type the newspaper is no longer an environment in which survival is the chief assignment. Today, newspapers are not merely a matter of cheap grey paper, thin ink and super-fast rotary printing, and type design no longer has to focus on surviving the mechanical technology and providing elementary legibility. Now there is also room to create an ambience, to give a paper a clearer identity of its own; there is scope for precision and refinement. One consequence of this is that newspaper designers can now look beyond the traditional group of newsfaces. (Conversely, a newsface can be used outside the newspaper — not an uncommon occurrence.)"

The same typeface can be used in very different ways, to different effect. As Unger himself has pointed out in talks at design conferences, his typeface Gulliver appears quite different in *USA Today* and in a contemporary German newspaper that also uses it as its text face. The American paper squashes the letters together, both vertically and horizontally, while the German paper gives them even more breathing room than Unger originally built into the fonts. In describing these two cases, Unger is diplomatically noncommittal about which one he prefers.

Colosseo	
Pantheon	→
San Paolo fuori le Mura	←
San Giovanni in Laterano	←

Gerard Unger designed Capitolium for a system of signage in Rome for the Jubilee Year (2000).

Fonts of the Eternal City

Among Unger's most recent type designs are two that he developed as signage typefaces for the Jubilee Year in Rome (2000): Capitolium and Vesta. He showed both typefaces and talked about the process of developing them when he spoke at the 2002 ATypI conference in Rome; ironically, the attendees of the conference could not go out and see his letters in use, because the exigencies of time and bureaucracy had meant that they had never gotten used. Unger had the foresight, however, to insist that the rights to the designs revert to him after the Jubilee year, so the two type families are now available directly from their designer.

Gerard Unger's website is not only a commercial source of well-designed fonts, it is a wealth of information on type design in general and his own designs in particular.

Feliciano Type Foundry

Typefaces from Portugal draw on surf-mag style, Fifties comics, and classic Spanish typographic roots.

[*May 30, 2003*]

As a display face, FTF
Morgan features strong,
simple forms and a variety of
weights and designs.

BS Mandrax, the most
extensive of Mário Feliciano's
funky "B-sides" type designs.

PORTUGUESE TYPE DESIGNER Mário Feliciano has a flair for big display and small text. The typefaces shown in *Feliciano Type Foundry: Specimen of Types* range from big, blocky display faces that recall the Constructivist designs of the '20s to carefully crafted serif and sans-serif faces that give style and readability to running text. It's a remarkable variety for someone who has been practicing type design for less than a decade.

Surf's up

"I started my career as a graphic designer," says Feliciano, "back in '93, as designer assistant in the leading Portuguese surf magazine, *Surf Portugal*. Since then I've been involved in its design, and many of my typefaces were developed to be used in it." He also had a rock band in the 1990s, and because of his connection to surf culture and rock music, "it's natural to me to have a more 'funky' and relaxed approach to type design."

If that were all Feliciano did, the typefaces he calls "B-sides" would make an interesting addition to the number of aggressively unsubtle headline faces available for magazine design, but it wouldn't be particularly remarkable.

"Then," says Feliciano, "there is the other side of my work — the more serious one."

Sans for text

Feliciano designed FTF Stella as a text face for *Surf Portugal*, which had always used sans-serif faces for text and resisted any change to a serif style. "I tried once to change to a seriffed face," he explains, "but we had very

Stella's forms recall some of the other popular humanist sans serifs, but don't duplicate any of them.

bad reactions from the readers, so I decided to create this sans with some characteristics of seriffed text faces."

What he created was a very clean, simple-looking sans serif that feels classical and reads comfortably in long text. It has a true italic, narrower and with italic letterforms, rather than the slanted roman that's common to many sans serifs. "I can't tell you any particular inspiration — the proportions are somehow based on my 'image' of roman type, much based on my study of [historical] Spanish types. I would say that W. A. Dwiggins's Metro or Fred Smeijers's Quadraat Sans might have played a role in here — but if you compare the typefaces, they are very different. I'm still missing some complementary versions (e.g., display or black) to make it more versatile."

FTF Stella is a text face designed for readers who don't like serifs but respond unconsciously to humanist letterforms.

> **There are approximately two billion**
>
> However, since Santa does not visit ch
>
> religions, this reduces the workload f
>
> or 378 million (according to the popul

The Morgan Project

Feliciano's largest type family so far is what he calls "The Morgan Project," an extensive set of sans-serif faces that cover both the biggest, boldest display and a stylishly techno form of text. The names suggest their uses: FTF Morgan Big is a family of fat all-caps display faces with sharp corners on the interiors of the letters and rounded rectangular forms on the outside; FTF Morgan Poster takes this idea and blows it up even further, condensing the letters a bit for poster use; and the remarkable FTF Morgan Tower takes an even more condensed form and then stretches it into three different heights with the same optical weight.

The text complement of FTF
Morgan holds its own at both
small sizes and small-display
sizes.

FTF *Morgan Sans has small
but significant differences
between the roman and the
italic designs.*

In contrast, or perhaps complement, to the big display forms there's the other half of the Morgan family: FTF Morgan Sans, a subtler, squarish sans serif text face with regular and condensed widths in two weights, and italics for the regular. Morgan Sans probably wouldn't work in really long passages of text, but in short text blocks it's very effective, and at small display sizes its crispness and the curved notches and rounded flaring of its construction — a sort of softened industrial look with a hint of the LCD screen — give it a very contemporary look. (It reminds me a bit of Sybille Hagmann's Emigre face Cholla — but without the "blurred" effect of Cholla. And when you look closely at the letterforms, they aren't that much alike.)

"Morgan is influenced by science fiction comics from the '50s," according to Feliciano. He started with the caps-only display type, and expanded it to all the versions shown in the specimen book — with more on their way. The design came from his desire to "mix some quite opposite concepts," he says. "The type is not calligraphic, but it is not completely mechanical either. And the variations, character sets, etc., show some respect for the typographic tradition. The 'italics' are deliberately called obliques, since they are a sloped version of the upright, optically corrected and with a change in the design of the lowercase **f**. People who like to have a design that looks 'up to date' can use Morgan and still be able to make a nice typographic job."

He adds: "It's becoming quite successful commercially."

Spanish sources

The subtlety evident in Feliciano's sans-serif designs shows itself to good effect in FTF Rongel, the first of several serif type families based on his studies of historical Spanish types. Rongel was a Spanish punchcutter in the second half of the 18th century, whose work is displayed, along with that of several other type designers, in a type specimen published in Madrid in 1799. Though Feliciano is from Portugal, he responds strongly to the style of these distinctive Spanish types. One of the most noticeable details of his Rongel revival is the sharp point of the bowl of the lowercase **a**.

Like Morgan, Rongel possesses a crispness that seems to suggest higher contrast than it actually has; the roman has a little of the sparkle that's so characteristic of Matthew Carter's ITC Galliard, and the hint of square internal corners in the counters gives the italic a complementary sharpness.

Well-displayed lines

Not insignificantly, in this specimen book, Mário Feliciano shows off his type designs very well. The juxtaposition of large, bold display sizes and variously shaped blocks of text provide enough variety of use to judge how effective they would be on the page. All the variations are labeled clearly but unobtrusively; I particularly like the way he indicates ligatures and alternate characters.

mechanics

Where type designs come from

Larry Brady invoked two thousand years of lettering as inspiration for type designers today, in a talk delivered at Zapfest only days after the events of Sept. 11, 2001.
[*November 9, 2001*]

A logo based on 1st-century Roman lettering, created by Larry Brady with a broad pen and later digitized.

WHERE DO TYPE DESIGNERS get their inspiration? That's the question that Larry Brady — calligrapher, type designer, graphic designer, and educator — spoke about in his lecture at the San Francisco Public Library during the series of talks and events collectively called Zapfest.

Brady's lecture, the second in the Zapfest series, was scheduled for the Saturday right after Sept. 11. When his flight from Los Angeles was canceled at the last minute, he and his wife Marsha decided to drive instead — a journey of several hundred miles and several hours on the road, each way. It was a commitment to carrying on that was admirable, but no one was sure until 2 p.m. on Saturday rolled around whether the audience would make the same commitment, in light of the week's traumatic events. At a few minutes before the hour it looked like the audience might consist of half a dozen people, but by starting time a sizable audience had collected. Since the best reply to destruction is construction and creation, this was a fitting way to respond. Zapfest itself was nothing if not a celebration of creation.

Need and desire

"It seems, in my limited knowledge, that the two primary motives for creating new typefaces are need and desire — or combinations of both," said Larry Brady at the beginning of his talk. "The need for new typefaces usually involves money, and since more than a few of my type-design friends have assured me that there is no money in designing type, I conclude that a lot of typefaces are created through desire."

Grid sketches for a square-cut uncial alphabet, originally created for a construction company.

Brady spoke about the origins of typography in the letters carved on the Trajan column in Rome, in the second century A D, and about how these letterforms have served as models and archetypes for letterers and calligraphers for nearly 2,000 years, and for type designers for the entire 500-year history of type. He cited Fr. Edward Catich, whose researches into how the Trajan letters were carved have ignited arguments and counter-arguments about just how and why those ancient Roman letters were created. "Edward Catich proposed," said Brady, "that ideal letters are universal prototypes, and being universal they exist only in the mind." (Catich's name and his ideas would come up repeatedly in later Zapfest lectures, both pro and con.)

2nd-century Roman fragments that show fine examples of Imperial Roman lettering.

Evolving forms on a solid structure
The inspiration for a new type design may come from anywhere in the historical record of written letters and printed type, but as Brady pointed out, any typeface has to have "an underlying armature upon which to build a design that can be recognized as alphabetic."

Brady alluded to the commonly understood development of roman typeface design until the 20th century when he said, "I have often thought that the history

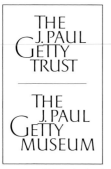

ABCDEFGHI
JKLLMNOPQ
RSTUVWXYZ
1234567890&
[!?$%¢£]
(.,;:/*˜ '''' «»)

THE
J. PAUL
GETTY
TRUST

THE
J. PAUL
GETTY
MUSEUM

*Alphabet (top) and
logos (above) created for
the Getty Museum.*

of typeface design beginning with the first types in the
15th century, through its 500 years of evolution, could
be arranged almost like a biblical passage: Jenson begat
Griffo begat Garamond begat Van Dijck began Janson
begat Caslon begat Baskerville and so on." Although he
points out that "in reality, type evolution was not quite
that linear," he says that "it would be safe to conclude
that the changes in type designs over time were not so
much in the underlying prototypical structures but in the
shapes built around this armature, with the three most
visible aspects of the type forms evolving consistently
in one direction: 1. the serifs became more refined and
delicate; 2. the contrast between thick and thin strokes
increased; and 3. the calligraphic or diagonal stress on
curves gradually disappeared as it moved to the vertical."

Letterforms for the Getty
Brady's own type designs include the titling font he
designed in the 1980s for the J. Paul Getty Museum in
Los Angeles. He was commissioned by Saul Bass to work
on the museum's identity, and went through an enor-
mously long and complex series of sketches, ideas, and
changing directions (which he detailed amusingly for his
San Francisco audience) before coming up with a typeface that took its inspiration from historical hand lettering as well as from the tapered, serif-less letters found in
some inscriptions in Renaissance Italy.

Brady felt that his own design was so close to Hermann Zapf's typeface Optima, which had some of the
same inspirations, that he suggested that the Getty simply use Optima. But Bass and the creative director, Dean
Smith, assured him that his designs were sufficiently
original to avoid confusion, and they wanted him to
develop a unique typeface for their use. Brady included
letters of varying heights, to give an option for visual
variety, but the overall effect is of a font of classic inscriptional capital letters.

Calligraphically derived logos.

Although the Getty planned a new identity when they moved into their new home atop a hill in Brentwood, in the 1990s, they ended up continuing to use Larry Brady's typeface for signage in the new location; the new logo, although varied in form, is clearly based on the same letters. "I was quite surprised to see the new logo direction for the new Getty," said Brady. He had been assured by Saul Bass, at the Aspen Design Conference in 1994, that while his design had worked just fine over the past ten years, it was "too recessive" for the Nineties. Imagine Brady's surprise when he saw his old letters in the newly designed logo.

A hands-on craft

In conclusion, Brady said that "there are probably as many approaches to the design of type as there are designers," but that "for myself, it begins with drawing or writing letters." While he could cite type designers, even some who are also calligraphers, who work directly onscreen to develop new typefaces, his own preference is to work first on "a good sheet of paper," in pencil or ink, and only later to transfer the letters into digital form. "There is," as he says, "a certain satisfaction in the making of something directly by hand."

Not your father's sans serif

Sans-serif typefaces can be more readable in text than most people expect — when they're based on traditional handwritten letters, like the growing number of "humanist" sans-serif typefaces.

[*July 22, 2002*]

THE RULE OF THUMB says that serif typefaces are easier to read than sans-serif typefaces, especially in running text. This isn't bad as rules of thumb go — it might help you narrow down the choice of typefaces when designing a book — but it's only a rough guide, not an ironclad rule. And it's often wrong.

In recent years, a whole slew of new sans-serif typefaces have appeared, many of them based on the same Renaissance handwriting as some of our classic serif text faces. Although they've been designed by many different people, and each typeface is different, they're sometimes grouped together under the name "humanist sans serifs." Sometimes this name is just a catch-all for anything without serifs that looks vaguely comfy and readable — as opposed to angular, mechanical, or geometric — but at heart it describes typefaces based on the humanist handwriting of 15th-century Italy, the manuscript hand that preceded our earliest roman (and italic) types.

Four different styles of sans-serif type (from left to right): a grotesque (HTF Knockout), a geometric (ITC Avant Garde), and two kinds of humanist sans serifs (Optima and Syntax).

Ogre Ogre Ogre Ogre

Despite the growing number of humanist sans serifs out there, they haven't gotten a lot of attention as a class. And type users still tend to think that all sans serifs are either funky 19th-century grotesques (that's the origin of Helvetica, though it's been spruced up and had its quirky bits smoothed down) or strictly geometrical ruler-and-compass constructions (the classic example is Futura — or, later and more exuberantly, Avant Garde).

Edward Johnston and Eric Gill

The tradition of humanist sans serifs isn't very old. It could be said to begin with Edward Johnston's "block letter" for the London Underground, which was introduced in the early 20th century. Johnston's inspiration was certainly calligraphic, but his typeface was designed for signage, and his capitals are based squarely on the ancient letters carved into Trajan's column in Rome.

More clearly humanist in form would be Eric Gill's eponymous Gill Sans, which is very similar to the Johnston letter in the roman (Gill had worked with Johnston) but also has a real italic. As many book designers since the 1920s have demonstrated, Gill Sans, if it's used carefully, can be a remarkably readable text face. (Today, in digital form, it has to be set a bit looser than the default letter-spacing in the digital fonts, in order to look the way it was intended to look.) The letters in Gill Sans are based on the letterforms of traditional roman and italic typefaces; but they have no serifs, and they are, generally, made up of strokes that all have the same thickness (or appear to).

Eric Gill's popular Gill Sans is a combination of humanist and geometric letter forms.

Whose typographer?

There is no reason why a sans-serif letter has to be monoline — that is, have only one thickness of stroke — but most of them are. It's part of the cult of simplification and streamlining that inspired radical designers early in the 20th century to take up sans serif as the "modern" letter form, the letter for the Machine Age. And there's undeniable power in that monoline form. It's unfussy, forthright, and simple; it holds the space in a way that few serif letters do. Even today, most humanist sans-serif typefaces show very little variation in the thickness of their strokes.

Optima and Syntax

Hermann Zapf's Optima, which he created in the 1950s, is often called a humanist sans serif, even though it's based not on handwriting but on the lettering carved into the floor of the church of Santa Croce in Florence. Optima is most certainly "humanist" in its spirit, and its letter forms are traditional text forms. Optima is famous for being a not-quite-sans; although it has no serifs, its strokes are subtly modulated, so that the ends of apparently straight strokes are slightly wider than the middle of the same strokes. (We often see this curvature exaggerated, today, in signage that uses Optima. The common signage typeface seems to be a version of Optima that was developed for early photo-typesetting systems, which would fill in the corners and make the stroke ends look round if the curves weren't increased to compensate. This compensation was done for text sizes, and for a typesetting technology that is now obsolete, but we're stuck with the same exaggerated letterforms on cheaply done signs all over the world.)

Hermann Zapf's Optima has no serifs, but its strokes are subtly curved and the underlying letter forms are traditional.

Whose typographer?

The first truly, deliberately humanist sans-serif typeface may have been Hans Eduard Meier's Syntax (released in 1968), which takes the letter forms of old-style serif faces such as Bembo or Garamond and translates them into an elegant monoline text face. There's a beauty to Syntax that makes you want to use it for text. I've seen it work especially well in conjunction with Sabon (a serif text face with similar forms), where the main text was in Sabon and ancillary material such as captions were in Syntax.

Whose typographer?

But I've always felt that there was something a little static about the elegance of Syntax, something that makes it wonderful for short text or in almost any kind of display use, but that doesn't quite pull the reader's eye forward when it's used in long blocks of text. Fans of that old rule of thumb would say that it's the lack of serifs that makes this so. (Syntax has recently been updated and expanded by Meier and Linotype, adding new weights and even a related serif version and an informal "letter" version for correspondence. But it has preserved one quirk of the original: no true italic, just a sloped version of the roman.)

Poised on the brink

This was the state of play, more or less, before the digital revolution in type. The humanist sans serif was an exotic animal, encountered only rarely, and not considered part of the mainstream of typographic development. But this has all changed. In the next essay, I take a look at some of the many humanist sans serifs now on the market, and try to figure out what makes them work.

The human side of sans serif

The last twenty years has seen an enormous growth in the number of humanist sans-serif typefaces — sans serifs designed for reading in text. Here are a few of the best.

[*August 5, 2002*]

WHEN A DESIGNER WANTS a humanist sans-serif typeface today, the choice is wide. As I've pointed out, there has been an explosion of sans serifs that are based on humanist handwriting and traditional text typefaces, rather than on strict geometry or on clunky 19th-century industrial forms. Where once the choices were limited to Optima, Gill Sans, Frutiger, and the ground-breaking Syntax, now there are so many entries in the "humanist sans" sweepstakes that the options are bewildering.

These are typefaces to be read. They may be drawn with only one thickness of line (although not all of them are) so that they stand foursquare on the page in the way that a modulated serif text face usually does not, and they may be stripped of serifs so that they look streamlined and somehow modern, but they have the forms we're used to in a typeface for reading. They fit together well — the best ones, anyway — and they flow along the line of text. Most of them have true italics, not just slanted versions of the roman letters, and the best include old-style figures and small caps, which are attributes of a text face.

A flowering of sans serifs
It's hard to know where to draw the line, between humanist sans serifs and other sans serifs that simply look good in text. After all, Futura was intended as a text face, and when it's spaced carefully it can look quite classical. But the typefaces I'm going to mention here are all relatively recent, and all firmly in the mold of the human-

ist sans. This is by no means an exhaustive list; it should, however, be a useful one.

One of the most readable sans-serif typefaces is The-Sans, the sans serif branch of the Thesis family, designed by Luc(as) de Groot. Thesis was originally released by FontShop, but the licensing rights reverted to de Groot and he now sells it directly, and licenses it to other font vendors. I first saw it used in the daily "newspaper" at one of the ATypI conferences, where it worked beautifully in narrow, unjustified columns. Since TheSans is somewhat narrow itself, it seems happiest in narrow columns, where it's most readable; in longer lines, although it still looks great, it becomes a little harder to read, requiring a little more effort. Its off-center alignment, in both roman and italic, reflects traditional letter forms and makes it particularly readable. In addition, when designing the fonts, de Groot took great care in how the letters fit together, and gave them a generously loose fit. The large number of alternate letters and special characters that de Groot has put into the character set also helps make it a good tool for setting text.

A detail of some text set in TheSans Semi Light and Semi Light Italic.

> In a certain reign there was a lady not of the rank whom the emperor loved more than any others. *The grand ladies with high ambitions her a presumptuous upstart, and lesser ladies still more resentful.* [TheSans Semi Light]

My personal favorite is FF Scala Sans, designed by Martin Majoor to complement his serif typeface, FF Scala. When I first saw samples of the unreleased typeface, I thought they must be just rough sketches; they looked so skeletal. But those were the final letterforms. They are skeletal — or perhaps elemental would be a better word — but they've got good bones. The letters are wide and spacious, the x-height is not too great, the curves are somehow both expansive and sharp, almost angular — just like Scala. In fact, since the regular weight of Scala is a somewhat light typeface, Scala Sans is in a way the more readable of the two in text. Because of its stark character, it's not right for every text situation, but it can function as a text typeface very well indeed. And its spaciousness works better in long lines than the narrow TheSans.

The same text set in FF Scala Sans, roman and italic, at the same point size and leading as the TheSans example.

In a certain reign there was a lady not of the fir rank whom the emperor loved more than any ₵ others. *The grand ladies with high ambitions tho a presumptuous upstart, and lesser ladies were st resentful.* [FF Scala Sans]

Adobe's Myriad, which was developed quite deliberately to be neutral in appearance, was designed collaboratively by Carol Twombly and Robert Slimbach. The roman looks a bit like Frutiger, though unlike Frutiger (at least until the arrival of Linotype Frutiger Next, a recent reworking of the family) Myriad has a true italic. The forms are round and simple, as befits a "neutral" sans, but they are firmly based on humanist letterforms; this gives them a readability beyond what the face's bland character might suggest. Like all of these sans-serif faces in text, Myriad should not be set with the letterspacing too tight.

Text set in Myriad Regular, roman and italic.

In a certain reign there was a lady not of the fir whom the emperor loved more than any of th *The grand ladies with high ambitions thought he presumptuous upstart, and lesser ladies were stil resentful.* [Myriad]

Stalking the wild Helvetica

Erik Spiekermann's FF Meta, and its many variants and spinoffs, didn't start off specifically to be a humanist sans serif; it started off to be simply legible, and the use of upright humanist letterforms was the way to achieve legibility. Meta is full of little details that take it away from the rigid, such as the flip to the top of the straight stroke in lowercase **n** and the varying angles at which the strokes are cut off. It's lively in a way that Helvetica is not. Meta is more typographic and less calligraphic than some of the more recent humanist sans serifs, but anyone looking at the lowercase **g** can see that this is meant to function as, among other things, a text face. I would have no hesitation about designing a book using Meta for the text type, if it had the right look and feel for the subject and the author.

In a certain reign there was a lady not of the fi
whom the emperor loved more than any of the
The grand ladies with high ambitions thought
presumptuous upstart, and lesser ladies were
more resentful. [FF Meta]

ITC Stone Sans, originally designed for Adobe by Sumner Stone, combines fairly round bodies with angular, stick-like arms, in a dance across the page that is inviting and readable in short passages; it may be a little too lively for quiet reading of a novel, say, but that liveliness makes it work in shorter texts. (The varying thicks and thins in the heavier weights add to the face's sparkle.) I often wish that somehow the timing could have worked out so that Stone Sans was the generic sans serif installed in the original Laserwriters instead of Helvetica; what an easier time we would all have had over the past decade and a half, in reading what comes out of office printers! (More realistically, perhaps, Charles Bigelow's earlier

Lucida Sans, one of the first typefaces designed for low resolution, using uncompromisingly humanist letterforms, would have made a good substitute. There's a definite resemblance between Lucida Sans and Stone Sans, to my eye. There is also some echo of this in Monotype's Ocean Sans, designed by Ong Chong Wah, especially in its lowercase **a**.)

The text in Stone Sans roman and italic.

In a certain reign there was a lady not of the rank whom the emperor loved more than a the others. *The grand ladies with high ambit thought her a presumptuous upstart, and les ladies were still more resentful.* [ITC Stone Sa

The Dutch connection

Fred Smeijers, who designed a very old-looking serif text face that is in fact purely digital in its inspiration and execution, FF Quadraat, later gave it a sans-serif companion, FF Quadraat Sans, which Smeijers described as "not just humanist but very humanist, and quite a character among the sanses." Like Quadraat, Quadraat Sans is narrow and a little spiky; in a block of text, it has less of the even color of most sans serifs.

One last time, the same text set in FF Quadraat Sans, and its unusually narrow, upright italic.

In a certain reign there was a lady not of the firs whom the emperor loved more than any of the c *The grand ladies with high ambitions thought her a pr tuous upstart, and lesser ladies were still more resentful* Quadraat Sans]

Michael Abbink's FF Kievit is another face designed to be smooth and neutral, but with a strong humanist basis. Kievit fits in the same quadrant of the typographic spectrum as Meta, but it has a different feel. (You may have noticed a certain preponderance of typefaces from

FontShop in this discussion. That's because FontShop has been in the forefront of developing and promoting humanist sans serifs, starting with Meta and continuing especially with typefaces from some of the young and once-young Dutch type designers who have investigated the humanist tradition.)

In a slightly different vein would be FF Profile, by Martin Wenzel, and Productus, by Petr van Blokland (the latter released by Font Bureau). Frank E. Blokland's DTL Haarlemmer Sans (Dutch Type Library) takes the forms of Jan van Krimpen's 1938 serif face Haarlemmer, which Blokland digitized in the 1990s, and turns them into a sans serif companion — something that van Krimpen himself was the first to do, though with another of his typefaces (Romulus). Jeremy Tankard's Shaker has some odd forms, like the **u** without a tail, but there's no doubt that it's humanist in inspiration and looks lively in text.

Unexpectedly familiar

Perhaps the most amusing example of a humanist sans-serif typeface would be Claude Sans, designed in 1988–90 by Alan Meeks for Letraset. It is quite simply a monoline, sans serif version of Claude Garamond's 16th-century French type — or rather, of the revivals based on Jean Jannon's 17th-century interpretation. Anyone who has used Monotype Garamond or Linotype's Garamond #3 will recognize the letterforms, and laugh. Claude Sans isn't a serious text face, but in small amounts, in the right circumstances, it becomes a witty commentary on serif vs. sans.

But wait! There's more! The wonderfully peculiar Claude Sans, set the same as the other samples.

In a certain reign there was a lady not of the first ran the emperor loved more than any of the others. *The ladies with high ambitions thought her a presumptuous up lesser ladies were still more resentful.* [Claude Sans]

The list goes on and on. Start scanning a catalog of new fonts with this criterion in mind, and you'll see innumerable examples. More to the point, try them out. Some of them won't work in running text, or not in the particular text you're trying to design, but some will. Readability isn't just a matter of serifs. Some very talented type designers have given us a wealth of new tools to work with; let's put them to use.

The front of the brochure for Neutraface shows the steel architectural letters and an outline of Richard Neutra's 1942 Boomerang chair.

Off the wall

Comparing a couple of sans-serif typefaces that both came from the lettering on buildings.

[*April 3, 2003*]

WHEN THE MOST RECENT typeface brochure from House Industries arrived, promoting their new release Neutraface, I gazed at the image of steel letters on a wall and thought of another sans-serif type family with its roots in signage: the Hoefler Type Foundry's Gotham. Both are geometric and almost aggressively simple in their design, and both date from the heyday of mid-century Modernism, which gives them a certain nostalgic appeal today. Both are inspired by clean, neutral, all-caps display lettering, but have been expanded into full type families with a lowercase, italics, and the attributes of text faces. It would be interesting, I thought, to compare the two.

Architect's rendering

Neutraface is based on the lettering found on some of the buildings designed by architect Richard J. Neutra. Unlike one of House Industries' earlier "sources," the imaginary fashion designer René Chalet, Richard Neutra is quite real; he died in 1970, and was a notable practitioner of Modern architecture. "His holistic approach," says the House brochure, "affected everything from his choice of building signage to the design of his furniture." (In typical House Industries fashion — these guys are masters of the collectible object — House hasn't confined itself to producing a typeface, but is also offering a line of Neutra Textiles, as well as "a reproduction of Richard's iconic Boomerang Chair" from 1942. "Now you don't need to own a Neutra home to enjoy a piece of Neutra history," they say.) Designer Christian Schwartz expanded the actual Neutra letters into a type family of five all-caps

House Industries' brochure makes use of metallic ink and spot varnish to give a layered effect in showing off Neutraface.

House Industries offers its Neutraface as stainless steel letters for use on buildings.

display weights, four text weights (with italics and even small caps), and two oddities based on Neutra's lettering from engineering diagrams.

House Industries even offers the individual letters from several of the Neutraface fonts as three-dimensional stainless-steel letterforms: "perfect for uses ranging from facade signage to typo-centric decoration." These are priced and marketed on the obvious assumption that you would only buy a few—enough for a house number, say, or initials—but you could use them for the signage of a large building, if you had the budget.

No-nonsense quality

The inspiration for Gotham isn't the work of a single iconic architect, but the lettering style common on buildings and signs throughout mid-century Manhattan. Tobias Frere-Jones celebrated his return to his native New York by designing a typeface based on the unnoticed everyday signage around him, starting with the lettering that labels the Port Authority Bus Terminal, the city's central hub for long-distance buses, a block west of Times Square.

"Like most American cities," writes Jonathan Hoefler about Gotham, "New York is host to a number of mundane buildings whose facades exhibit a distinctively American form of sans serif. This kind of lettering occurs in many media: the same office buildings whose numbers are rendered in this style, in steel or cast bronze, often use this form of lettering for their engraved cornerstones as well. Cast iron plaques regularly feature this kind of lettering, as do countless painted signs and lithographed posters, many dating back as far as the Works Project Administration of the 1930s. And judging by how often it appears in signs for car parks and liquor stores, this might well be the natural form once followed by neon-lit aluminum channel letters.

The Gotham samples bring to mind the visual cacophony of vernacular signage on the streets of New York.

275 MADISON AVENUE
McKim, Mead, and White

CHRYSLER BUILDING
Abraham David Beame

The sample phrases used in the Gotham specimen evoke the names and buildings of New York City.

Gotham is designed to work in both display and text settings.

"Although there is nothing to suggest that the makers of these different kinds of signs ever consciously followed the same models," Hoefler goes on, "the consistency with which this style of letter appears in the American urban landscape suggests that these forms were once considered in some way elemental."

Frere-Jones took these "plainspoken and practical alphabets of shop windows and billboards" and turned them into a four-weight type family of upper- and lowercase with italics for each weight, plus four weights of a condensed version (with a lowercase but without italics). (Perhaps the Hoefler Type Foundry missed a good bet by not working out an arrangement to offer neon signage based on Gotham. Or would that be redundant?)

A native New Yorker, Tobias celebrates his return to the city with **Gotham,** this new family of typefaces. Gotham takes both its name and its inspiration from a form of public lettering common to New York, and indigenous to the United States. These letters

The inflections of nostalgia

The presentation of the two different type families reflects the styles of the two different type foundries. House Industries' approach is always consciously, flamboyantly retro, with a smooth, seamless presentation that evokes an era. The Hoefler Type Foundry's look is more traditionally typographic; their publications hark back to the best type-specimen books of the past, even when the typeface they're displaying is based on Times Square signage rather than Renaissance calligraphy. Both foundries, in their different ways, have a knack for making you want to get your hands on their fonts and put them to use.

The actual letterforms, especially in the capitals, are similar between the two typefaces: rounded, generous proportions; uniform thickness of strokes; extreme sim-

The Hoefler Type Foundry catalog uses just two extra colors in a collage of imagined uses for Gotham.

plicity of form; and the suggestion that they were drawn by an engineer. The ends of curved strokes in both faces are cut off diagonally, straight across the stroke, rather than horizontally or vertically; but diagonal straight strokes all end horizontally. Letters like **O** and **C** are near-circles, while **S** falls into a more natural, somewhat lazy pair of loops (in Neutraface a bit rounder than in Gotham). In both faces, the **M** has straight legs, and its diagonal strokes meet well above the baseline. The **K** in both faces has a bottom leg that springs from the top leg, rather than straight from the stem, and the leg of the **R** drops down from the loop. But the looping counter of **P** and **R** can be rounder in Neutraface, because it reaches farther down the stem.

This is one of the primary differences between the two designs: Neutraface has a low midline, with the center bar of **E** and **F** and the cross-stroke of **A** coming very far down the letter, giving Neutraface a slightly Art Deco feel. This is carried through to the lowercase, which has a very low x-height. Gotham, by contrast, has its midline near the optical center of the capital letters, and its lower-case has a large x-height. In text, Neutraface tends to suggest Futura, even though it's less obviously geometric, while Gotham evokes the strong but faceless public lettering of the 1950s.

Neutraface includes fonts designed specifically for text, with a small x-height and two-storey a's and g's.

The Neutra Legacy

Richard J. Neutra (1892-1970) was arguably among the most important architects of the Modern era. His holistic approach affected everything from his choice of building signage to the design of his furniture. House Industries is honored to be part of his continuing legacy.

For more on the Neutra oeuvre visit www.neutra.org

ILLUSTRATION AT RIGHT: Reunion House (Dion Neutra House), 1949-50, Los Angeles

The Gotham type family, unlike Neutraface, includes a highly condensed version.

Both typefaces are carefully spaced to work either in all-caps display or in upper- and lowercase text. Round forms like these need breathing room, especially in the lighter weights (both families include a Light, and Neutraface includes an even lighter Thin), so it's important to set the default letter-fit of the fonts loose enough. Both foundries have done this.

There and back again

These typefaces complete the circle between lettering and type. They are digital fonts based on physical lettering that appeared on buildings long before the digital era, and they will undoubtedly be put to use in print in a great variety of ways: in magazines, advertising, brochures, captions, maybe even books. But in a period when more and more physical signage is created from digital fonts, these typefaces may also end up on signs in shop windows and lettering on building facades, right next to their original sources of inspiration. It would be strangely fitting.

Then and now

Ten years ago, the classic typeface of Seventies advertising design, ITC Avant Garde, was released in a new form: as a multiple master font, the malleable format pioneered by Adobe. But where is it now?
[*May 1, 2003*]

As I WAS rummaging through back issues of *Upper & lowercase*, researching images and ideas for a book on *U&lc* (published in 2004 by Mark Batty Publisher), I came across an ad in the 20th-anniversary issue (vol. 20, no. 1; Spring, 1993) that caught my eye. It was a two-page spread announcing that, on May 17, 1993, ITC Avant Garde would be available in Adobe's new multiple master font format.

   That date is almost exactly ten years ago. Looking back on it a decade later prompts all kinds of reflections about the interplay of typographic fashion and font technology. Both fashion and technology change quickly; it would be hard to say, in the digital world, which one is more transient.

Multiple master technology could create almost infinite variations of a typeface.

MULTIPLE MASTERS

Yesterday's tomorrow

ITC Avant Garde already had a long history in graphic design, from its origins in the creatively explosive days of the late Sixties. The text of the 1993 *U&lc* ad is of course marketing copy, but it accurately places the typeface in its context: "Throughout its 25-year life, ITC Avant Garde has lived up to its name by continually breaking new ground. It began as Herb Lubalin's logo for the always innovative, and often controversial magazine, *Avant Garde*. It then became the first typeface released by ITC when the company was founded in 1970. Because of its large x-height, extensive set of alternative and ligatured characters and strong design personality, the face also broke new stylistic ground for typeface creation. Now ITC Avant Garde is the first ITC typeface to be issued as a multiple master Type 1 typeface."

Multiple master technology, which in the early Nineties was the Next Big Thing, is notoriously hard to explain in words and static images, but wonderfully easy to demonstrate by dragging a slider back and forth onscreen. As you drag the slider, the letterform you're looking at morphs: from fat to thin, for instance, or from condensed to expanded, depending on how it was designed to change. The slider is moving along the font's "axis"; there's a different version of the letter at each end of the axis (Extra Fat at one end, say, and Really Thin at the other), and as you drag the slider along the axis you can create any variation in between those two extremes. The technology behind this is more complicated (and the possibilities are really quite sophisticated), but it's easy to see how it works in practice. The point is that the typeface designer creates those master designs at the ends of the axis, and determines just how the letter shapes will change as the slider is dragged. If the font has a width axis, then you can widen or narrow the letters without seeing the distortions in shape and stroke width that appear when you simply stretch or squeeze the type. The result is better-looking type.

And a multiple master font can have up to three different axes, each of them changing the typeface in a different way. The multiple master version of ITC Avant Garde, for instance, had two axes: weight and width. So you could make everything from a very light, condensed version to a very heavy, expanded version — or, for that matter, from light and expanded to heavy and condensed.

The ad explained the potential uses of these options: "Now type in headlines and body copy can be exactly the proportions you want. Headlines can be customized subtly or dramatically in weight or width to precisely fit virtually any measure. Type in blocks of text copy can be adjusted subtly or dramatically to achieve just the color desired. Or type can be manipulated to compensate for the inherent differences in the appearance of type printed using various technologies, such as lithography, Xerography or gravure."

Malleable geometry

ITC Avant Garde was an odd choice for turning into a multiple master typeface. The original design was strictly geometric, based on large, perfectly round counters and curves, and short straight lines. Even creating a condensed version (which Ed Benguiat did in 1974) was a difficult enterprise; when the circle becomes a narrow oval, the whole character of the typeface changes. What would it be like if you could generate any degree of condensed or expanded letters that you wanted? Wouldn't it look a little odd, if they were all mixed together?

ITC Avant Garde was a quintessentially 1970s typeface, created by Herb Lubalin and Tom Carnase for the kind of "expressive typography" practiced in the New York advertising world at the time. It was made for tight layouts and boldly conceived headlines. I can only speculate on what Lubalin would have thought of the infinite malleability of a multiple master typeface, or what he would have done with it. He might have been delighted, or he might have been appalled. He would certainly have used its possibilities in extremely creative ways.

One of the problems of ITC Avant Garde is that it takes a typographer of Lubalin's skill to use it well. It's extremely easy to use Avant Garde badly — all the more so if you try to emulate that 1970s style of composition. The multiple master version only gave us an even wider range of potential disaster.

A detail of the 1993 ad in
U&lc for the upcoming
multiple master version of
ITC Avant Garde.

The tool not used

But only if people would actually put it to use. I have no idea how well ITC Avant Garde multiple master sold, either then or later, but the multiple master technology never took off with the majority of type users. And that's a shame. It had the potential to revolutionize how type got set, and to improve the quality of everyday type to an enormous degree. But it fell between the cracks of the software development process.

Multiple master became an esoteric technique for advanced type users (I've used multiple master typefaces extensively in books and other kinds of graphic design), but what it should have been was an intuitive tool for the masses. If every Adobe application had incorporated a simple interface for generating multiple master "instances," and if popular business applications like Microsoft Word or Excel had been designed to automatically choose the appropriate font instance, then multiple master technology would have proliferated, seamlessly and invisibly — and the quality of everyday, ordinary typesetting would be a lot better than it is today.

But to have this happen would have required that the software development teams working on all these products, both within Adobe and in other companies, recognize the importance of this font technology. And, for the most part, they didn't. Multiple master seemed superfluous, a specialist's toy, rather than a core technology for manipulating type wherever it's used. So instead of incorporating an easy way to use multiple master fonts in each application, they forced users to "generate an instance" — one that was named with a ridiculous string of numbers and letters, which might describe it technically but meant nothing to anyone trying to use the font — and only then would that particular version of the typeface be available for use in the application. If the user wanted a slightly different version (more condensed, say, or a different optical size), they'd have to go generate that instance, too, before they could use it. This was a magnificently cumbersome way to work, and not surprisingly very few people bothered.

A chance missed

Today, multiple master technology is all but dead. A couple of years ago, Adobe stopped officially supporting it — which means, in effect, that there's no guarantee that a multiple master font will work properly in new versions of Adobe applications. (Not to mention any other company's programs.) Some of the subtleties of the better-designed multiple master typefaces (like optical sizes) have been carried over to the newer OpenType font format, but without the infinite variation that multiple master's design axes made possible. The only place where the technology still appears is in Adobe Type Manager, which uses the multiple master fonts Adobe Serif and Adobe Sans to mimic the character widths of missing fonts in a document.

And ITC Avant Garde? It's still in wide use, though perhaps not in its multiple master version. Indeed, over the last few years, it's had a revival, thanks to the popularity of the Retro Seventies look in graphic design. It's still hard to use well, but it still provides designers with another tool for creative typography.

INDEX